# You Really Don't Look 50, Charlie Brown

# You Really Don't Look

# Charlie Brown

RR
RAVETTE PUBLISHING

PEANUTS comic strips: © 1957-1999 United Feature Syndicate, Inc.
Based on the book 'You Don't Look 40, Charlie Brown!'

This edition published in the Year 2000 by Ravette Publishing Limited,
Unit 3, Tristar Centre, Star Road, Partridge Green, West Sussex  RH13 8RA

Printed and bound in Great Britain by CPD Wales, Ebbw Vale

ISBN: 1 84161 020 8

A cartoonist is someone who has to draw the same thing day after day after day without repeating himself.

*I probably spend more time than is good for me either reliving or regretting the past, but that kind of thinking is partly what cartoons are made of. For this anniversary book, I wanted to write something a little bit different, so here are a few thoughts and recollections that have inspired, either directly or indirectly, some comic strips and Sunday pages. This is not the answer to the much asked question of where ideas come from, for I really can't answer that, but it does suggest how some of the prompting comes about.*

Charles M. Schulz

My earliest recollection of drawing and getting credit for it and being complimented on it is from kindergarten. I think it was my first day, and the teacher gave us huge sheets of white paper, large black crayons, and told us to draw anything we wanted. I drew a man shoveling snow, and she came around, paused, looked at my picture, and said, "Someday, Charles, you're going to be an artist." Now she wasn't quite right— she didn't say "cartoonist"—but there was an interesting aspect to this. I had drawn the snow shovel as a square, but I knew this was not right. I knew nothing about perspective, and didn't know how to fix it, but I knew that something wasn't right about this picture. I like to think there was some anticipation there of what was to come.

When I was in the first grade, the teacher put a valentine box on a table in front of the room. It was two days before Valentine's Day and we were to bring to school the cards we wanted to give to the kids we liked. Obviously, there were some I liked more than others, but because I didn't wish to offend anyone, I made out a list that included everyone. My mother helped me select all the cards, and I took them to school the next day. Classrooms are pretty big to a first grader, and it was a long walk from where I sat up to the front of the room where the valentine box waited. Everyone could watch you as you walked to the front of the room and dropped each card through the slit on top of the box.

I couldn't do it. I took all the valentines home.

CHARLIE BROWN, I'VE BEEN FEELING AWFULLY GUILTY ABOUT NOT GIVING YOU A VALENTINE THIS YEAR...I'D LIKE FOR YOU TO HAVE THIS ONE

HOLD ON THERE! WHAT DO YOU THINK YOU'RE DOING? WHO DO YOU THINK YOU ARE?!

WHERE WERE YOU FEBRUARY 14th WHEN EVERYONE ELSE WAS GIVING OUT VALENTINES? IS KINDNESS AND THOUGHTFULNESS SOMETHING YOU CAN MAKE RETROACTIVE? DON'T YOU THINK HE HAS ANY FEELINGS?!

YOU AND YOUR FRIENDS ARE THE MOST THOUGHTLESS BUNCH I'VE EVER KNOWN! YOU DON'T CARE ANYTHING ABOUT CHARLIE BROWN! YOU JUST HATE TO FEEL GUILTY!

AND NOW YOU HAVE THE NERVE TO COME AROUND A WHOLE MONTH LATER, AND OFFER HIM A USED VALENTINE JUST TO EASE YOUR CONSCIENCE! WELL, LET ME TELL YOU SOMETHING... CHARLIE BROWN DOESN'T NEED YOUR...

DON'T INTERFERE...I'LL TAKE IT!

The living rooms in the homes of our friends when we were little varied a good deal. They looked different and they smelled different. Some we were allowed to play in. Others we only walked through. Some we never saw at all. If the home contained an older sister, we never talked to her. Older sisters were awesome.

HAVE YOU EVER NOTICED HOW CERTAIN HOMES HAVE DISTINCT COOKING ODORS?

YOU MEAN LIKE GARLIC OR SPAGHETTI?

I KNOW ONE KID'S HOUSE THAT ALWAYS SMELLS LIKE THEY'VE BEEN COOKING CABBAGE

OURS SMELLS LIKE TV DINNERS!

---

CHARLIE BROWN SAYS THAT BROTHERS AND SISTERS CAN LEARN TO GET ALONG...

HE SAYS THEY CAN GET ALONG THE SAME WAY MATURE ADULTS GET ALONG...

AND HE SAYS THAT ADULTS CAN GET ALONG THE SAME WAY THAT NATIONS GET ALONG...

AT THIS POINT THE ANALOGY BREAKS DOWN!

MADAM FULLCHARGE

YOU DON'T THINK MY BROTHER AND I GET ALONG VERY WELL, DO YOU?

YOU JUST WAIT....SOMEDAY, AFTER WE'RE GROWN, WE'LL BE VERY CLOSE!

WHAT DOES SHE MEAN BY "CLOSE"?

WE MAY BOTH LIVE ON THE SAME CONTINENT!

LUCY, DEAR SISTER!

I ALMOST BOUGHT YOU A BIRTHDAY PRESENT JUST NOW

I SAW THIS BOTTLE OF COLOGNE IN A STORE WINDOW, AND IT ONLY COST A DOLLAR...

I KNEW IT WOULD MAKE YOU HAPPY TO GET IT, BUT THEN I SAW SOMETHING THAT I KNEW WOULD MAKE YOU EVEN MORE HAPPY!

IN THE WINDOW OF THE STORE NEXT DOOR, THERE WAS A SALAMI SANDWICH WHICH ALSO COST A DOLLAR...NOW, I KNOW HOW CONCERNED YOU ARE FOR THE PEOPLES OF THIS WORLD...

I KNOW HOW HAPPY IT'S GOING TO MAKE YOU WHEN I BECOME A FAMOUS DOCTOR, AND CAN HELP THE PEOPLE OF THE WORLD

BUT IF I'M GOING TO BECOME A DOCTOR, I'M GOING TO HAVE TO GET GOOD GRADES IN SCHOOL...

AND TO GET GOOD GRADES, I'M GOING TO HAVE TO STUDY, AND IN ORDER TO STUDY, I HAVE TO BE HEALTHY...

IN ORDER TO BE HEALTHY, I HAVE TO EAT...SO INSTEAD OF THE COLOGNE, I BOUGHT THE SANDWICH...ALL FOR YOUR HAPPINESS!

I'M SO HAPPY I COULD CRY!

HERE...I BROUGHT YOU A PIECE OF TOAST

WELL, THANK YOU

"THANK YOU, DEAR SISTER"

THANK YOU, DEAR SISTER

"THANK YOU, DEAR SISTER..GREATEST OF ALL SISTERS"

THANK YOU, DEAR SISTER..GREATEST OF ALL SISTERS!

"THANK YOU, DEAR SISTER, GREATEST OF ALL SISTERS, WITHOUT WHOM I'D NEVER SURVIVE!"

THANK YOU, DEAR SISTER, GREATEST OF ALL SISTERS, WITHOUT WHOM I'D NEVER SURVIVE!

YOU'RE VERY WELCOME

HOW CAN I EAT WHEN I FEEL NAUSEATED?

When I was in the sixth grade, there would frequently be interruptions in our class as a particular boy was suddenly ordered to go to the principal's office. Soon he would return with a nice grin on his face, wearing a striking leather belt with an attached shoulder strap and a silver badge. Everyone in the class would applaud, for it meant that he had been chosen to be on the school patrol. I never achieved this honour, probably because I was not considered forceful enough, and was also either the smallest or the next-to-the-smallest kid in class. I did get to be substitute, however, but that never rated the leather Sam Browne belt. Girls were never chosen. Somehow, not being chosen bothered me only a little. I simply decided that I was not quite good enough, and let it go at that. It would have been nice, though, to have walked into the class with that leather belt.

**ME?** YES, MA'AM... CALLED TO THE PRINCIPAL'S OFFICE, EH, MARCIE?

WHAT DID YOU DO? C'MON, YOU CAN TELL ME...

I DIDN'T DO ANYTHING! I'M INNOCENT!

YOU SHOULD HAVE SLEPT MORE IN CLASS, MARCIE.. YOU GET IN LESS TROUBLE THAT WAY!

A PATROL PERSON?!? THEY MADE YOU A PATROL PERSON?!!!

ISN'T IT EXCITING? I'VE ALWAYS WANTED TO BE ON THE SCHOOL TRAFFIC PATROL... IT'S A VERY GREAT HONOR...

YOU'RE NOT JEALOUS, ARE YOU, SIR?

JEALOUS? HOW COULD ANYONE POSSIBLY THINK I'M JEALOUS?

GUESS WHAT, CHUCK... THEY MADE MARCIE A PATROL PERSON!

CAN YOU IMAGINE THAT? CAN YOU REALLY IMAGINE THAT, CHUCK?

WELL, I DON'T KNOW... SHE'S A VERY GOOD STUDENT.. I SUPPOSE SHE DESERVES IT...

I HATE TALKING TO YOU, CHUCK!

MA'AM, HOW COME MARCIE GOT TO BE A SCHOOL PATROL PERSON AND I DIDN'T?

I'D DO ANYTHING TO BE A PATROL PERSON...

I'D STAND OUT IN THE SUN, OR THE RAIN OR THE SNOW! I'D DIRECT TRAFFIC IN AN EARTHQUAKE! I'D DO ANYTHING!!

STUDY?!

$$2,956 - 743$$

MARCIE, I DON'T NEED YOU TO HELP ME ACROSS THE STREET!

RULES ARE RULES! I'M THE PATROL PERSON, AND I'LL TELL YOU WHEN YOU CAN GO ACROSS!

ALL RIGHT, EVERYBODY, LET'S GO! QUICKLY NOW! TO THE OTHER SIDE! QUICKLY NOW! QUICKLY!

STOP

IT'S ONLY THREE O'CLOCK, BUT AS SOON AS I GET HOME, I'M GOING TO BED!

---

WHY SHOULD MARCIE GET TO BE A PATROL PERSON AND NOT ME?

I CAN'T STAND IT!

THIS IS NOT LIKE ME..

I'M INTO JEALOUSY, CHUCK!

YOU LOOK TIRED, MARCIE

I AM, SIR.. I GOT UP AT SIX O'CLOCK SO I COULD BE AT MY PATROL POST ON TIME

I'M SO SLEEPY... I DON'T THINK I CAN STAY AWAKE MUCH...

...LONGER... Z

I used to own the very first copy of *Famous Funnies* that was ever published. I don't have the slightest idea what happened to it. Other comic magazines began to imitate *Famous Funnies*, and I bought every one that came out. One of the stores lost me as a customer, however, when the man behind the counter said to me once too often, "Going to do some heavy reading, eh?"

THIS IS WHAT I ENJOY.. A MID-AFTERNOON SNACK...

I THINK I LIKE CEREAL MORE IN THE AFTERNOON THAN I DO IN THE MORNING...

NOW, I HAVE TO FIND SOMETHING TO READ WHILE I EAT MY COLD CEREAL, AND I HAVE TO FIND IT FAST BEFORE THE CEREAL GETS SOGGY...

I CAN'T STAND TO EAT COLD CEREAL WITHOUT HAVING SOMETHING TO READ..

RATS! SOMEBODY TOOK THE SPORTS SECTION OUT OF THE MORNING PAPER! AND WHERE'S THE FUNNIES? THEY TOOK THE FUNNIES, TOO! GOOD GRIEF!

"MOBY DICK"...NO, I DON'T WANT TO START THAT RIGHT NOW..."THE INTERPRETER'S BIBLE"....TWELVE VOLUMES...THAT'S A LITTLE TOO MUCH FOR ONE BOWL OF CEREAL..."BLEAK HOUSE"...NO..."JOSEPH ANDREWS"...NO..

THIS IS TERRIBLE! I'VE GOT TO FIND SOMETHING FAST!

COMIC MAGAZINES! HAVE I READ ALL OF THEM?

I'VE READ THAT ONE, AND THAT ONE, AND THIS ONE, AND THAT ONE, AND THIS ONE, AND THIS ONE, AND...

I HAVEN'T READ THIS ONE!

SOGGY!

I can't remember if I was in the eighth or ninth grade, but I do know that in one of those art classes I learned the most important lesson of my life about creativity. Each year when one of the professional ice shows came to St. Paul, art students were given a chance to compete for free tickets by creating posters advertising the shows. I drew a very good Popeye those days and could letter quite well. The other kids in class mostly drew either a man or a woman skating. My poster showed Popeye skating and my poster lettering was, in my mind, much superior to all the others and, especially, that of Stanley, the young fellow who sat next to me and who had drawn, of all things, a polar bear coming out of an igloo. What in the world did that have to do with an ice show?

"Your poster is really neat, Charles," the kids would say to me. "You're going to win for sure." I didn't, of course, for the judges saw something original in Stanley's polar bear compared to all the other dull skating figures and copied Popeyes. It was a good lesson.

**WHAT'S THIS?** OH, IT'S JUST A LITTLE PICTURE I DREW OF A MAN ON A HORSE...

OH, I JUST LOVE HORSE PICTURES!

COULD I HAVE IT, CHARLIE BROWN? COULD I HAVE IT TO HANG ON MY WALL?

WELL, I GUESS SO... IF YOU THINK IT'S GOOD ENOUGH...I MEAN.. AND HOW ABOUT SIGNING IT? WILL YOU SIGN IT, TOO? WILL YOU PUT YOUR NAME ON IT?

ALL RIGHT..WHAT DO YOU WANT ME TO DO...JUST SIGN MY NAME, OR... YOU WERE GOING TO DO IT, WEREN'T YOU?

HA!HA!HA!HA! HA!HA!HA!HA!

YOU REALLY THOUGHT I WANTED TO HANG THIS STUPID PICTURE ON MY WALL, DIDN'T YOU? HA!HA!HA!HA!

..AND HE EVEN THOUGHT I WANTED HIM TO SIGN IT! HA!HA!HA!HA!

I CAN'T STAND IT!

Most of our baseball games were pickup games with guys from other neighbourhoods, although for one summer when I was fourteen we had an organized four-team league due to the arrangements of our local playground director. Unlike today's Little League, parents were virtually nonexistent as spectators, but during this same fourteen-year-old summer we began playing softball games in the evening after we had all had dinner (or as we called it in the midwest, "supper"). One of the fathers would frequently join these games, and because he was a pleasant fellow and played quite well, we always welcomed his presence and, in fact, envied the kid who had such an athletic father. Not that we were at all critical of our own fathers, for we were well aware of the difficulties of the Depression, and knew how hard they worked, but still, the envy was there. A few years later we discovered that this man's marriage was very shaky, and he was probably only too happy to get out of the house and play softball with the kids after dinner.

TWO OUTS ALREADY.. I CAN'T STAND IT!

OKAY, LUCY, WE NEED A RUN..HERE'S WHAT I WANT YOU TO DO...

IF YOU GET ON FIRST, WATCH FOR MY SIGNAL TO STEAL SECOND...I'LL TUG MY EAR LIKE THIS...

NOW, IF YOU GET TO SECOND, AND I WANT YOU TO STEAL AGAIN, I'LL CLAP MY HANDS LIKE THIS...

IF YOU GET TO THIRD, AND I WANT YOU TO STAY THERE, I'LL TUG MY OTHER EAR LIKE THIS, BUT IF I WANT YOU TO TRY TO STEAL HOME, I'LL RUB THE FRONT OF MY SHIRT...

STRIKE ONE!

STRIKE TWO!

STRIKE THREE!!

THAT WAS EASIER THAN TRYING TO REMEMBER ALL THOSE SIGNALS!

HEY, MANAGER! I'M MAKING OUT OUR LINEUP...SEE WHAT YOU THINK..

I'VE GOT SCHROEDER DOWN FOR CATCHER, LINUS AT SECOND BASE AND SNOOPY AT SHORTSTOP...

HOW ABOUT DH? WHO'S OUR DESIGNATED HITTER?

I PUT DOWN SHERMY, OKAY?

THAT'S FINE...SHERMY'S A GOOD HITTER

AND I'VE PUT YOU DOWN FOR DG

DG?

DESIGNATED GOAT!

HOLD IT!

HOLD IT!

WHAT'S THE MATTER?

BEFORE WE START THE GAME, CHARLIE BROWN, YOU HAVE TO ASK THE BALL IF IT WANTS TO PLAY..

I HAVE TO **WHAT?**

YOU HAVE TO ASK THE BALL IF IT WANTS TO PLAY! YOU ASKED THE OTHER TEAM, DIDN'T YOU? AND YOU ASKED ALL OF YOUR OWN PLAYERS, DIDN'T YOU? OF COURSE, YOU DID!

NOW, YOU HAVE TO ASK THE BALL! AFTER ALL, THE BALL IS THE ONE WHO'S GOING TO GET HIT ALL THE TIME, ISN'T IT? DON'T YOU THINK IT SHOULD HAVE A CHOICE?

GO AHEAD, CHARLIE BROWN...ASK THE BALL.. ASK THE BALL IF IT WANTS TO PLAY...

I FEEL LIKE A FOOL

HEY, BALL..DO YOU WANT TO PLAY IN THE GAME TODAY?

IT DIDN'T ANSWER

IT'S TRYING TO MAKE UP ITS MIND...I GUESS I'LL GO HOME...

GO HOME?!

I'M NOT GOING TO STAND AROUND ALL DAY WHILE SOME STUPID BALL TRIES TO MAKE UP ITS MIND!

SCHULZ

The opening day baseball game at Lexington Park in St. Paul was always cause for excitement, and for some reason those of us who wanted to attend were released from school early. I was a junior in high school at the time, and was only too willing to accept this legitimate opportunity to avoid afternoon classes. Strangely enough, not many took advantage of this break, but I still remember getting to the park early and seeing a girl from our school come down the aisle and sit near me. What intrigued me was a large notebook she opened wherein she had ruled out in pencil a complete box score preparatory to keeping track of the plays of everyone in the game. Something about the diligence of a young girl who, because she obviously could not afford to buy a real scorecard, had so carefully made her own, saddened me. I should have talked to her, but I didn't have the nerve.

The Park Theatre was a movie house across the street and down about a half block from my dad's barbershop. The changing of attractions was always fascinating, even though they were regular. One feature ran on Sunday and Monday. The next ran from Tuesday through Thursday, and the next on Friday and Saturday, with a matinee and serial on that last afternoon. I always liked coming out of the theatre at night after the last show and seeing one of the ushers standing on a ladder changing the letters that spelled out the next attraction. When I was eight years old, my mother took me to my first Saturday matinee. The serial was called *The Jade Box*, and I remember only two scenes; some men in an open touring car dressed in formal wear trying to escape from someone, crashing through a wooden road barrier. In the other scene, some blood seeped under the wall from one room to another.

On succeeding Saturdays we also saw Rin Tin Tin and some Bobby Jones shorts. After the latter, I asked my mother to buy me a golf club. It was a niblick, a toy, of course, with a head made out of lead. I took it onto the playground that was across the street from where we lived, and having no golf balls, began to hit small pebbles. A tiny friend lined the pebbles up for me, and all went well until he placed one in the line that was a bit too large, and the club head broke. It was another seven years before I got to play a real game of golf.

Amos and Andy were at the height of their popularity on radio. We never missed listening at nine o'clock each evening. One night in the middle of a movie, my mother and dad began discussing something, and then leaned toward me and whispered, "Which would you rather do, see the rest of the movie, or go home and listen to Amos and Andy?" We went home to the radio.

Several years later, I imagine when I was about ten, the theatre advertised a free Butterfinger candy bar to the first one hundred kids attending that Saturday's matinee. I stood in line and as I approached the box office, saw the last candy bar disappear. I was the one-hundred-and-first!

When I was nine or ten, and my parents would go out someplace, my grandmother and I would go to the theatre that was right around the corner. After the comedy short, and maybe one of those pieces I hated, with an orchestra playing on screen, they would have either Paramount News or Movietone News. The newsreel would always finish with "The End," and I was always afraid my grandmother would say, "Well, let's go home!" I would invariably turn to her and say, "Grandma, that just means that the news is over and the movie is about to begin," and she would always say, "Yes, I know." It took me about forty years to realize that grandma was a lot smarter than I thought she was.

*Deer*

THAT SHOULD BE "DEAR"

IN THE SALUTATION OF A LETTER, THE PROPER WORD AND SPELLING OF THAT WORD IS "DEAR"

*Deer are beautiful animals found in most parts of the world.*

I'M SORRY... I DIDN'T REALIZE YOU WERE WRITING ABOUT DEER... I APOLOGIZE...

WELL, I SHOULD HOPE SO! IT SEEMS TO ME THAT A LOT OF THE PROBLEMS IN THIS WORLD ARE CAUSED BY PEOPLE WHO CRITICIZE OTHER PEOPLE BEFORE THEY KNOW WHAT THEY'RE TALKING ABOUT!

*Dear Grandma,*

SCHULZ

DECEMBER 25

DEAR GRAMPA AND GRANDMA,

WHAT ARE YOU DOING?

THANK YOU FOR THE CHRISTMAS PRESENT.

ARE YOU TRYING TO MAKE ME LOOK BAD?

I WAS REAL HAPPY TO GET THE DOLLAR.

YOU'RE WRITING A "THANK YOU" NOTE RIGHT AWAY JUST TO MAKE ME LOOK BAD, AREN'T YOU?

IT WAS VERY THOUGHTFUL OF YOU.

YOUR KIND DRIVE ME CRAZY! WHY DO YOU HAVE TO BE SO EFFICIENT?! WHY DO YOU HAVE TO...

LUCY ENJOYED HER GIFT, TOO, AND SAYS TO THANK YOU VERY VERY MUCH.

!

LOVE, Linus

IF YOU'LL WAIT A MINUTE, I'LL RUN AND GET YOU AN AIR MAIL STAMP!

I never knew either of my grandfathers and only one grandmother, Sophia Halverson, my mother's mother, who lived off and on with us most of my life. To me, she was always an old lady, although it could very well be that I am now as old as she was when she first lived with my mother, dad, and me. She was much wrinkled, had increasing hearing problems, was always dependant on her children, and suffered one of the worst tragedies that can come to a mother; she outlived six of her nine children. She loved sports, but knew almost nothing about the real details of any. When Patty Berg became prominent in the Minnesota golfing area, my grandmother always checked the papers to see if Patty had won, although she had to ask me which was the better score, a high one or a low one.

Our house had a typical Minnesota basement with an open area beneath the stairs. The space beneath the stairs and the supporting post was about six feet and made a pretty good facsimile of a hockey goal. Being very accommodating, my grandmother would take a broom that I gave her and stand in front of this make-believe goal while I shot tennis balls at her with a hockey stick. I like to think she made a lot of great saves.

---

---

---

I'VE TOLD YOU A MILLION TIMES THAT ADULTS ARE DIFFERENT!

YOU HAVE TO BE ABLE TO READ THEM..

YOU KNOW WHAT YOUR TROUBLE IS? YOU JUST DON'T UNDERSTAND THE ADULT MIND..

I CAN PREDICT WHAT THE AVERAGE ADULT WILL SAY OR DO IN ALMOST ANY GIVEN SITUATION...

THIS IS A MUST IF YOU ARE GOING TO SURVIVE AS A CHILD!

NOW, TAKE GRANDMA, FOR INSTANCE...I CAN PREDICT EXACTLY WHAT SHE WILL SAY IN THE FOLLOWING SITUATION....

YOU DRAW A PICTURE AND I'LL DRAW A PICTURE...THEN YOU TAKE THE TWO PICTURES IN, AND SHOW THEM TO GRANDMA...

ASK HER WHICH PICTURE SHE THINKS IS THE BETTER..I PREDICT THAT SHE WILL LOOK AT THEM AND SAY,"WHY, I THINK THEY'RE BOTH VERY NICE"

GRANDMA, HERE ARE TWO PICTURES THAT LINUS AND I HAVE DRAWN..WHICH ONE DO YOU THINK IS THE BETTER?

WHY, I THINK THEY'RE BOTH VERY NICE

YOU JUST HAVE TO UNDERSTAND THE ADULT MIND!

Dear Grandma,
How are you? I am fine.

I have been working hard in school.

WHICH GRANDMA ARE YOU WRITING TO? WE HAVE TWO GRANDMAS, YOU KNOW...

I AM WELL AWARE OF THAT! I AM ALSO AWARE THAT THEY DON'T LIKE EACH OTHER...

AND THAT BRINGS UP A PROBLEM...

WHICH GRANDMA GETS THE PHOTOCOPY?

FANTASTIC!

HAVE YOU EVER KNOWN ANYONE WHO HAS THE GIFT OF PROPHECY?

JUST MYSELF

YOU?!

ABSOLUTELY! I CAN PREDICT WHAT ANY ADULT WILL ANSWER WHEN HE OR SHE IS ASKED A CERTAIN QUESTION

IF YOU GO UP TO AN ADULT, AND SAY, "HOW COME WE HAVE A MOTHER'S DAY AND A FATHER'S DAY, BUT WE DON'T HAVE A CHILDREN'S DAY?" THAT ADULT WILL ALWAYS ANSWER, "EVERY DAY IS CHILDREN'S DAY!"

IT DOESN'T MATTER WHAT ADULT YOU ASK... YOU WILL ALWAYS GET THE SAME ANSWER...IT IS AN ABSOLUTE CERTAINTY!

I'LL TRY IT OUT ON GRANDMA...

GRANDMA, HOW COME WE HAVE A MOTHER'S DAY AND A FATHER'S DAY, BUT WE DON'T HAVE A CHILDREN'S DAY?

EVERY DAY IS CHILDREN'S DAY

THE GIFT OF PROPHECY!

Children do not converse. They say things. They ask, they tell, and they talk, but they know nothing of one of the great joys in life, conversation. Then, along about twelve, give or take a year on either side, two young people sitting on their bicycles near a front porch on a summer evening begin to talk about others that they know, and conversation is discovered. Some confuse conversation with talking, of course, and go on for the rest of their lives, never stopping, boring others with meaningless chatter and complaints. But real conversation includes asking questions, and asking the right questions before it is too late.

In 1980 I was part of a panel that was requested to appear before four hundred exceptional high school students. Each of us on the panel was to talk for only a few minutes on any subject that we thought appropriate. Some talked of the greatness of our country; one dragged out a standard anticommunist speech, but all tried to say something that might be of use to the young people in the audience. My turn was coming up, and I still hadn't decided what useful thing a cartoonist had to contribute other than the trite recommendations of dedication and hard work. Something else had been working its way forward in my mind, however, in recent weeks, and I decided to gamble on it even though it was very personal to each listener.

"I am not one to give advice," I said, "and always hesitated to do so with my own children, but tonight I am going to give you some advice that is very important . . ." I then told them to go home and begin asking questions of their parents, to stop saying things to their parents, and instead begin asking things about their parents' pasts that demonstrate a real interest, and pursue the questioning. "Don't stop until you have learned something about your father's first job or your mother's early dreams. It will take energy, but it will be infinitely worthwhile, and it must be done now. It must be done before it is too late."

I didn't exactly get fired from a job I had working in a grocery store when I was eighteen, but I was certainly "let go." As a clerk, I was utterly hopeless. I never knew the price of anything, and never developed the skill of being really useful. I was a good delivery boy, however, and almost enjoyed filling the miserable truck that was all the owners could afford, and driving around certain areas of St. Paul delivering the groceries to homes sometimes guarded by barking dogs. One Chow dog refused ever to let me near the house. Another Irish setter got into the bag of groceries that I left on the back steps of a house where no one answered the doorbell. The grocery store was a small one on the front edge of a red brick apartment complex. One of the customers was a beautiful dark-haired housewife who was probably in her early twenties. She always answered the door in a sheer dressing gown. She also was the only one who ever gave me a tip for delivering the groceries. After paying me what she owed, she always gave me a nickel. The job ended suddenly on a Saturday afternoon when one of the women who was part owner of the store paid me my regular nine dollars and said they really didn't need me anymore. It didn't bother me a bit.

During my senior year in high school and for most of the next year, I took the lessons of the Federal Schools' correspondence course. I didn't always have the right drawing paper, and soon learned that the stiff white cardboard used by the laundry when they returned shirts was not really suitable for good pen and ink work. Actually, I learned a good deal from the correspondence course, and after "graduating" used to drive from St. Paul over to Minneapolis where the school was located, to get personal criticism from Frank Wing. His style was of the old school, and he had difficulty explaining to me why my style was still not appropriate. It is very hard to explain to a young person why the supposedly crude drawings in Popeye were actually wonderful. I tried sending in gag cartoons, but collected only form rejection slips.

One day, my mother suggested that perhaps my cartoons weren't "smutty" enough. She chose the word carefully, and I believe accurately for that day. My problem, however, was that I couldn't have drawn a "smutty" cartoon if I had tried. One day, I answered an ad for a "junior artist." It was a direct mail advertising firm in downtown Minneapolis. The boss had me fill out a questionnaire that called for a couple of simple drawings, and amazingly enough, I found myself hired as a "junior artist." Unfortunately, the title was a ruse to get a delivery boy. When I asked the lady who was in charge of getting material delivered throughout the downtown area when I was going to get to do some drawing, she said, "Oh, no, he did it again! He hires young guys as 'junior artists' when he only wants delivery boys!"

At the end of the first pay period, I took my money to a local department store and bought a cartoon collection called *Colliers Collects Its Wits*. During the lunch hour, I sat at a table looking through the book when the other young fellow who was not an artist, but actually a bona fide delivery boy, asked me what I was reading. It was beyond his comprehension. He could not understand why anyone would pay two dollars and fifty cents for a book of cartoons.

I went through two more delivery boy jobs before finally ending up at another direct mail advertising firm in downtown St. Paul, where I worked in a small room with four other young men tying bundles of tabloid-size papers together. We did this from eight until four-thirty, and for the first few days, I thought I would lose my mind. But almost all jobs have some kind of satisfaction to them, and we soon developed pride in our speed and dexterity in tying up the bundles.

Also, there were two charming girls in their early twenties, named June and Marie, who sometimes sat at a table in our room addressing labels. I found that I could laugh and joke with them, and discovered the wonderful feeling for the first time in my life of being liked.

Eventually the owners of the business found out that I could draw and do lettering. They began to let me work on mimeograph layouts drawing simple cartoons. In between these projects I also made deliveries around town. The company did well for itself. It got a cartoonist and a delivery boy for sixteen dollars a week.

The gag writer was also developing. One day just before the new year, I was assigned the task of going around the downtown area on foot to deliver the new firm calendars to all their best customers. When I left the office, the foreman told me to call back in after an hour or so to see if they needed me for anything. After working my way from building to building, I soon found myself several miles from our office with a light snow falling. I called back as ordered, and the foreman asked, "Where are you?"

"I'm not sure," I said. "All I know is I just saw a buffalo walk by!" The gag writer (or smart aleck) was on his way.

After the war, my first job was doing free-lance lettering for comic magazines where everybody else did the drawing. I lettered not only in English, but in French and Spanish too, even though I didn't know those languages. I would do them sitting in my kitchen at night after my regular job was over. Then I'd get up early, drive downtown to St. Paul, leave off the pages I had lettered, and drive to my regular job. Did I regard having to work two jobs as a hardship? No! I regarded it as something great. I was involved. I was doing something with cartoons.

Whenever I am asked about the origin of the name "Peanuts," I always manage to slip in a little dig that it is the worst name ever thought of for a comic strip. The original title was to have been "Li'l Folks," (admittedly, not much better) but "Tack" Knight, the creator of "Little Folks," a strip that was no longer running, asked us not to use our title because he thought he might someday revive his characters.

Larry Rutman of United Feature Syndicate, who was eventually to become one of my very best friends, and treated me almost like a son or nephew, or something, called me and said we needed a new title. All I could think of was "Charlie Brown," or "Good Ol' Charlie Brown." The syndicate people didn't care for those, and then informed me that they had the perfect title, "Peanuts." I was horrified, and called Larry immediately and told him it was a terrible title. It was undignified, inappropriate, and confusing. I said that readers would almost certainly think it was the name of the lead character, and that no one ever referred to small children as "peanuts."

"Well," he said, "the salesmen are ready to take the feature on the road, and we think it's a title that will catch the attention of editors." What could a young unknown from St. Paul say? I gave in. Years later, I was told by Bill Anderson, their production manager, that he had been asked to try to think of a title for a new kid strip United was about to launch so he wrote a list of ten possibilities, one of which was "Peanuts." He said he had never seen the strip.

About three years later I was visiting New York, and was taken by Larry Rutman for lunch at the weekly meeting of the Dutch Treat Club. I remember Victor Borge as being the afternoon entertainer. At one point, the regular members passed little cards up to the chairman indicating who their guests were. He looked at the cards, read off the names, and as each guest stood, made some remark. "Larry Rutman," he said, "has as his guest today Charles Schulz, the creator of 'Peanuts.' Now isn't that a hell of a thing to be the creator of?!" I turned to Larry and said, "See?"

When I began to draw the kids in the strip really talking to each other, or maybe thinking about something, the obvious pose was sitting on a curb much the way the characters in the early *Skippy* strips by Percy Crosby were drawn. Almost immediately, however, and maybe because I had children of my own, I became sensitive about showing them sitting where they could easily be hit by a car. Eventually I developed the brick or sometimes stone wall, and showed them behind it leaning on their arms staring out at the world.

One day I started to build a stone wall myself behind our driveway at home as kind of a therapeutic exercise. It was not at all beautiful and certainly had no useful purpose other than to get me out in the sun and make me feel that I was really doing something. As the wall began slowly to take shape, my wife, Jeannie, came out to look at it and remarked, "That looks just like the wall you draw in the strip!"

I NEVER SEEM TO KNOW WHAT'S GOING ON...

RIGHT FROM THE VERY START MY LIFE HAS BEEN STRANGE

I THINK I KNOW WHAT HAPPENED..

I MUST HAVE MISSED ALL THE REHEARSALS

---

I'D LIKE TO MAKE A LOT OF MONEY, BUT I'D HATE TO BE A SNOB..

I'VE GIVEN THIS A LOT OF THOUGHT

SO WHAT HAVE YOU DECIDED?

SO I'VE DECIDED TO BE A VERY RICH AND FAMOUS PERSON WHO DOESN'T REALLY CARE ABOUT MONEY, AND WHO IS VERY HUMBLE BUT WHO STILL MAKES A LOT OF MONEY AND IS VERY FAMOUS, BUT IS VERY HUMBLE AND RICH AND FAMOUS..

GOOD LUCK!

---

SO I DON'T KNOW WHICH PROGRAM TO WATCH... MAYBE I'LL JUST READ A BOOK, WHO KNOWS? I ALSO HAVE A LOT OF PHONE CALLS TO MAKE

WHEN SCHOOL STARTS AGAIN, THERE'LL BE OTHER THINGS TO DO, I SUPPOSE..LIFE GOES ON, I GUESS, DOESN'T IT?

WELL, IT'S BEEN NICE TALKING TO YOU, CHARLIE BROWN..

THANK YOU..IT'S BEEN NICE LISTENING

---

MY HEAD HURTS

YOU SHOULD GO SEE YOUR DOCTOR

HOW MUCH DO YOU SUPPOSE HE'D CHARGE?

WHO KNOWS? MAYBE YOUR WARRANTY IS STILL GOOD!

**I GUESS IT'S WRONG ALWAYS TO BE WORRYING ABOUT TOMORROW**

**MAYBE WE SHOULD THINK ONLY ABOUT TODAY...**

**NO, THAT'S GIVING UP...**

**I'M STILL HOPING THAT YESTERDAY WILL GET BETTER**

---

**DID YOU EVER STOP TO THINK THAT EVERY DAY IS SOMEBODY'S BIRTHDAY?**

**NO MATTER WHAT DAY IT IS, SOMEBODY IN THE WORLD HAS THAT DAY FOR A BIRTHDAY!**

**HAVE YOU EVER THOUGHT ABOUT THAT, CHARLIE BROWN?**

**NO, I CAN'T REALLY SAY THAT I HAVE...**

**YOU'RE GOING TO HAVE TROUBLE WHEN YOU GET TO COLLEGE!**

---

**LIFE IS A LOT LIKE A BASEBALL GAME**

**WE ALL HAVE CERTAIN POSITIONS THAT WE PLAY**

**WE ALL MAKE A FEW HITS AND WE ALL MAKE A FEW ERRORS**

**HOW MANY INNINGS ARE WE PLAYING?**

---

**JUST BEFORE THE TEST BEGAN, OUR TEACHER GOES,"DOES EVERYONE HAVE A PENCIL?"**

**THIS FAT KID ACROSS THE AISLE FROM ME GOES," I DON'T!"**

**THEN THIS OTHER KID WITH THE GLASSES GOES,"SURE YOU DO... YOU HAVE MINE!"**

**WHATEVER HAPPENED TO THE WORD "SAID"?**

I don't know why there's so much unrequited love in my strip. I seem to be fascinated by unrequited love, if not obsessed by it: Sally loves Linus, Linus can't stand her; Lucy loves Schroeder, Schroeder can't stand her; Charlie Brown loves the red-haired girl, but doesn't even dare to go near her. There's something funny about unrequited love—I suppose it's because we can all identify with it. We've all been turned down by someone we love, and it's probably the most bitter blow in life.

YOU KNOW WHAT?

I ALWAYS ENJOY SPECULATING ON WHAT OUR LIFE WOULD BE LIKE IF YOU AND I EVER GOT MARRIED, SCHROEDER...

I'LL BET WE'D HAVE A SON..AND HE'D PROBABLY BE A GREAT MUSICIAN JUST LIKE YOU...

BUT I WONDER WHAT HE'D LOOK LIKE... I WONDER IF HE'D HAVE MY SENSITIVE EXPRESSION...

WHAT DO YOU THINK OUR SON WOULD LOOK LIKE?

WELL, PERHAPS.....BUT I'D LIKE TO THINK THAT HIS NOSE WOULDN'T BE QUITE THAT BIG...

SCHULZ

**Panel 1:** DID YOU SEE MY "SWEET BABBOO" STANDING THERE?

**Panel 2:** HE'S HANGING AROUND THE CANDY STORE TRYING TO DECIDE WHAT TO GET ME FOR VALENTINE'S DAY...

**Panel 3:** IT'LL PROBABLY BE A BOX OF CANDY SHAPED LIKE A BIG HEART...

**Panel 4:** OR A BIG **ZERO**! / ISN'T HE THE CUTEST THING?

**Panel 1:** LOOK! DO YOU SEE THAT? / SEE WHAT?

NOTHING, THAT'S WHAT!! THERE'S NOTHING TO SEE BECAUSE IT'S A MAILBOX WITH NO VALENTINES IN IT, WHICH IS NOTHING TO SEE!!!

**Panel 3:** MY SWEET BABBOO DIDN'T SEND ME A BOX OF CANDY OR A VALENTINE OR ANYTHING

I SEE WHAT YOU MEAN.. THERE'S NOTHING TO SEE... / SEE?!

---

**Panel 1:** SALLY, GET UP! YOU'RE GONNA BE LATE FOR SCHOOL!

**Panel 2:** LINUS DIDN'T SEND ME A VALENTINE, AND HE BROKE MY HEART AND I'M NEVER GOING TO SCHOOL AGAIN!

**Panel 3:** AND IF YOU SEE MY SWEET AN' SOUR BABBOO, PUNCH HIM IN THE NOSE!

**Panel 4:** "SWEET AN' SOUR"?

**Strip 1:**

Panel 1: WHAT'S THIS? THAT LITTLE RED-HAIRED GIRL DROPPED HER PENCIL...

Panel 2: GEE... IT'S GOT TEETH MARKS ALL OVER IT...

Panel 3: SHE NIBBLES ON HER PENCIL...

Panel 4: SHE'S HUMAN!

**Strip 2:**

Panel 1: WHAT'S THAT YOU'RE HOLDING?

Panel 2: IT'S A PENCIL... IT BELONGS TO THAT LITTLE RED-HAIRED GIRL... I'M GOING TO STAND HERE UNTIL SHE WALKS BY, AND THEN I'M GOING TO TELL HER HOW I FOUND IT...

Panel 3: I HATE TO SEE YOU GO TO ALL THAT TROUBLE, CHARLIE BROWN... WHY DON'T I JUST GIVE IT TO HER?

Panel 4: HEY! HERE'S YOUR STUPID PENCIL!!

**Strip 3:**

Panel 1: WOULDN'T IT BE SOMETHING IF THAT LITTLE RED-HAIRED GIRL CAME OVER HERE AND GAVE ME A KISS?

Panel 2: I'D SAY, "THANK YOU! WHAT WAS THAT FOR?" AND WOULDN'T IT BE SOMETHING IF SHE SAID, "BECAUSE I'VE ALWAYS LOVED YOU!"

Panel 3: THEN I'D GIVE HER A BIG HUG, AND SHE'D KISS ME AGAIN! WOULDN'T THAT BE SOMETHING?

Panel 4: WOULDN'T IT BE SOMETHING IF IT TURNED OUT THAT FRENCH FRIES WERE GOOD FOR YOU?

**Strip 4:**

Panel 1: YOU SHOULD GO OVER AND TALK WITH THAT LITTLE RED-HAIRED GIRL, CHARLIE BROWN

Panel 2: ASK HER TO EAT LUNCH WITH YOU

Panel 3: TELL HER YOU'D BE HAPPY JUST TO BE WITH HER FOR AN HOUR OR SO

Panel 4: AN HOUR? I'D SETTLE FOR AN "OR SO"!

For years, I have wanted to draw a tender, bittersweet story about Charlie Brown and the little red-haired girl where I would actually show her, but I don't think it will happen. She will probably always remain an off-stage character, for no matter how often I try, I simply can't draw her.

Several years after the *Peanuts* strip had begun running, my Dad admitted to me that he had had doubts about my being able to think of enough ideas to keep it going. This, in spite of the fact that he was always typically proud of everything I did. One day when I was eighteen, a painting contractor came into my dad's shop, and while getting his hair cut, he began to talk about his latest job which was the redecorating of one of the finest restaurants in downtown St. Paul. He said everything seemed to be relatively easy, but he was puzzled as to what he should do about the large mural that wound its way behind the bar and out into the main dining room and around the walls. He needed someone who knew something about art and oil painting to come in and "jazz it up." My dad proudly recommended me.

I knew as much about oil painting as I did cutting hair. In the correspondence course in cartooning and illustrating that I had been studying, there was a one-page article on how to paint with oils. This had been included merely to satisfy student curiosity, for the course dealt only with the commercial side of art. I actually set up an easel of sorts one day, and tried to follow the instructions that said to begin with a simple subject such as flowers, which I did. About halfway through the painting, it fell off the easel and landed face down on the carpet, and that was the last time I tried to paint anything. Now, however, I was being interviewed by the painting contractor who had returned for another haircut.

"Sure," he said, "why don't you come on down and try it. We'll give you all the stuff you need. We have brushes and paint. You'll have your primary colours. Come on down and see what you can do." Just the way he said "You'll have your primary colours" told me that he didn't know any more about this project than I did, and that I was in trouble. That night, however, I made the trip downtown and went first to a late movie to kill time before reporting to the restaurant after its midnight closing time. When I walked in, I saw a lot of activity as waiters were clearing up the evening dishes and painters were setting up scaffolding and stirring paint in big buckets. And there was the mural. Pioneers crossing America. Covered wagons, desert, brave souls facing the West all done in various shades of what could only be described as "brown."

"That's our problem," the painting contractor said. "It's just too drab. It's too dull now for the rest of the place. See what you can do to brighten it up." I looked at the mural for a few minutes trying to decide what to do. I should have looked at the door. One of the painters came over and asked if I needed any help. I told him that I thought I might begin by painting the sky a light blue, so he very cheerfully set about mixing up a shade that seemed appropriate; and with a two-inch brush that he gave me I climbed the scaffolding and started high in one corner to "brighten up the mural."

On the second night, I tried adding some streaks of red to indicate a setting sun, and amazingly enough, the painters would come by every now and then, and say, "That sure looks a lot better than that ugly brown." My progress with the two-inch brush on this huge mural was very slow. I had completed only about twenty feet by the third night, and when I walked in, I saw two regular painters filling in the sky areas around the heads of the pioneers. "I think we can handle the rest of it by ourselves," the painting contractor said to me. "Why don't you just figure out what I owe you?" I consulted with my dad about what would be a fair price. When I asked him what the minimum wage was, he told me twenty-five cents. I sent the painting contractor my bill for six dollars.

I'M DRAWING A ROW OF TREES, AND I'M GOING TO COLOR THEM GREEN

THAT'S NOT ART

I'LL PUT A LAKE IN FRONT OF THE TREES

THAT STILL WON'T MAKE IT ART

AND BY THE LAKE I'LL DRAW A TINY LOG CABIN

THAT'S NOT ENOUGH...YOU NEED A WATERFALL AND A SUNSET...SHOW THE SUN GOING DOWN SORT OF ORANGEY, AND PUT SOME RED STREAKS IN THE SKY, AND HAVE SOME SMOKE COMING OUT OF THE CHIMNEY

NOW PUT IN SOME MORE TREES...MAKE IT A FOREST... AND HAVE A DEER STANDING BY THE WATERFALL... THAT'S RIGHT...

NOW YOU HAVE TREES, A LAKE, A LOG CABIN, A WATERFALL, A DEER AND A SUNSET...

THAT'S ART!

SOMETIMES IT TAKES A LAYMAN TO SET THESE PEOPLE STRAIGHT

I have to admit that I don't like it when people come up to me with a three-year-old in their arms, point me out to the child and say, "Do you know who this is? This is Snoopy's father!"

An elderly couple was sitting at the table next to me in the ice arena coffee shop one morning. I noticed that she kept glancing at me, and finally she said, "I don't want to bother you, but I think I recognize you. Aren't you Snoopy's father?"

"No," I said.

"Oh, I'm sorry. You looked familiar."

"I'm Charles Schulz," I said. "And I draw Snoopy, but I'm not his father."

WHAT ARE YOU THINKING ABOUT, CHARLIE BROWN?

AM I WRONG OR DID THERE USED TO BE MORE TREES THAN THERE ARE NOW?

THEY SAY THAT WHEN THE COLONISTS FIRST CAME TO THIS COUNTRY, A SQUIRREL COULD TRAVEL TREETOP TO TREETOP FROM THE ATLANTIC TO THE MISSISSIPPI RIVER WITHOUT EVER TOUCHING THE GROUND...

BONK! BONK!

EITHER THAT WAS A LONG TIME AGO, OR THAT WAS SOME SQUIRREL!

SCHULZ

Why dogs are superior to cats.

They just are, and that's all there is to it!

SHORT AND TO THE POINT!

---

Beauty Tips

How to look younger...

Don't be born so soon.

SLEEPING AGAIN

I DON'T SEE WHY YOU NEED SO MUCH REST

I NEED PLENTY OF REST IN CASE TOMORROW IS A GREAT DAY..

IT PROBABLY WON'T BE, BUT IF IT IS, I'LL BE READY!

It was a dark and stormy night.

Once upon a time, it was a dark and stormy night.

HERE'S THE FIERCE JUNGLE ANIMAL PERCHED IN A TREE READY TO POUNCE ON A VICTIM WHO PASSES BELOW..

WHAT CAN YOU EXPECT FROM SOMEONE WHO GRADUATED AT THE BOTTOM OF HIS CLASS AT POUNCE SCHOOL?

After fifteen years of drawing Snoopy sitting at his little portable typewriter, I started a strip and completely forgot how to draw the typewriter.

"A Guide to Running"

Chapter One

How to run like a rabbit.

Hop Hop Hop
Hop Hop Hop

---

"Help!" she cried.

"Help! Help! Help!
Help! Help! Help!"

THIS IS A VERY BORING STORY...

I'LL ADD ANOTHER "Help!"

---

"I can't tell you how much I love you," he said.

"Try," she said.

"I'm very fond of you," he said.

"Nice try," she said.

---

HAVE YOU EVER TRIED WRITING A PLAY?

MAYBE YOU COULD BECOME ANOTHER WILLIAM SHAKESPAW!

HAHAHAHA!

BONK!!

This Sunday page was inspired by the memory of a strange high-command order—an order whose short life was proof of its impracticality. A few weeks after the Sunday page appeared, I was astounded to receive a letter from a retired colonel who proudly announced that he was the officer who originated the regulation. Apparently, it was an attempt to solve an epidemic of athlete's foot by forcing the men to change shoes and socks each day. He admitted to receiving much "good natured ribbing" as he travelled in the field with an inspection team. I couldn't resist telling him that we had always regarded it as one of the dumbest orders ever received. Now, I feel guilty for telling him that. It's hard to answer letters every day, however, without sometimes getting a little carried away.

Outside of drawing comic strips I think the thing that makes me the most happy is producing one of our professional ice shows at the Redwood Empire Ice Arena, which my wife and I built. It opened in 1969, and is regarded as literally the world's most beautiful ice arena. Every other year we produce a professional ice show, starring the greatest ice skaters in the world. For me to stand by the railing, watching these marvelous skaters rehearse, is happiness.

WHAT ARE YOU PRACTICING FOR NOW, SIR?

I'M WORKING ON MY THIRD-TEST FIGURES, MARCIE... SOMEDAY I'LL BE IN THE OLYMPICS...

THAT WOULD BE EXCITING, SIR..WOULD YOU INTRODUCE ME TO DICK BUTTON?

I'D EVEN INTRODUCE YOU TO MR.FRICK

RIGHT ON, SIR!

---

WHAT DO YOU THINK OF MY FORWARD LOOPS, COACH?

GROWL, SNARL, SNAP, GROWF, BARK, WOOF!

ARE ALL SKATING COACHES AS CRABBY AS YOU?

GROWL, SNARL, SNAP, GROWF, BARK, WOOF!

---

HOW MANY SKATING TESTS ARE THERE, SIR?

EIGHT, MARCIE, AND THEY GET HARDER AND HARDER

SOMETIMES I THINK THE ONLY THING THAT KEEPS ME GOING IS THE ENCOURAGING WORDS OF MY COACH...

GROWL, SNARL, SNAP, GROWF, BARK, WOOF!

---

OKAY, BEAUTIFUL, GET OFF THE ICE!! WE'RE GONNA PLAY HOCKEY!

HOCKEY?! GET LOST, NECKHEAD! I WAS HERE FIRST!!

YOU WOULDN'T LIKE TO GET HIT WITH A HOCKEY STICK WOULD YOU, BEAUTIFUL?

HOW WOULD YOU LIKE TO BE FORCE-FED A PAIR OF GOALIE PADS?!

I DON'T EVEN REMEMBER WHAT HAPPENED, SIR...

WELL, THOSE HOCKEY PLAYERS WERE ABOUT TO GIVE ME A ROUGH TIME, AND YOU CAME RUNNING OUT TO HELP ME, MARCIE

BUT I SLIPPED AND FELL ON THE ICE, HUH?

I'LL SAY YOU DID!

LET'S GO BACK AND SHORTEN A FEW LIFE SPANS, SIR!

LATER, MARCIE, LATER

---

GUESS WHAT, SIR...WHEN I GOT HOME AND TOLD MY MOTHER ABOUT FALLING ON THE ICE, SHE CALLED THE DOCTOR...

HE TOLD YOU TO TAKE IT EASY, HUH? WELL, THAT MAKES SENSE..CAN I GET YOU ANYTHING?

NO, THANK YOU, SIR... I'M JUST GOING TO LIE HERE, AND TRY TO READ "PILGRIM'S PROGRESS"

IF THE FALL ON THE ICE DIDN'T GIVE YOU A CONCUSSION, MARCIE, THAT WILL!

I'M AFRAID I'M GOING TO BE A DISAPPOINTMENT TO YOU, MARCIE...

I WENT OVER TO THE RINK TODAY TO GET REVENGE ON THOSE HOCKEY PLAYERS

DID YOU PUNCH THEIR LIGHTS OUT, SIR?

I WAS GOING TO, MARCIE...

BUT THEN THEY ASKED ME TO PLAY CENTER ON THEIR TEAM!

I studied and passed the required tests to become a referee for amateur junior hockey at all levels from age five to twenty. Several friends and I became very conscientious and dedicated referees and linesmen (in spite of what the fans in the stands and certain players might say). In hockey officiating, it is required that the referee throw his left arm into the air when he is about to whistle a penalty. It becomes so ingrained that as soon as a player commits an infraction such as tripping, slashing, or elbowing an opponent, your arm immediately goes up. The blowing of the whistle then follows. After years of refereeing, this action has become completely automatic to me. One day I was walking through a department store and saw one shopper accidentally jostle and trip another. My left arm started to shoot into the air. Fortunately I was not carrying a whistle.

A friend of mine told me once how her young son had come home from school one day, burst through the door, hurled his jacket down on the couch, and moaned, "Mom, I feel just like Charlie Brown." He didn't have to say anything more. She knew exactly what he meant. And when someone says "She's a real Lucy!" you know who they're talking about. I suppose this is one of the things that cartoon characters can do for us—to define feelings that we can't necessarily express ourselves.

**Panel 1:** PSYCHIATRIC HELP 5¢ / THE DOCTOR IS IN / I THINK YOU SHOULD WORK HARD TO IMPROVE YOUR CHARACTER CHARLIE BROWN...

**Panel 2:** ONCE A CHILD GETS TO BE FIVE YEARS OLD, YOU KNOW, HIS CHARACTER IS PRETTY WELL ESTABLISHED / THE DOCTOR

**Panel 3:** BUT I'M ALREADY FIVE YEARS OLD! I'M **MORE** THAN FIVE! / THAT'S RIGHT, YOU ARE AREN'T YOU?

**Panel 4:** TOO BAD...THAT'S THE WAY IT GOES! / THE DOCTOR IS IN

---

**Panel 1:** I THOUGHT HAVING A BABY SISTER WOULD CHANGE MY WHOLE LIFE, BUT IT HASN'T.

**Panel 2:** PEOPLE STILL HATE ME..NOBODY **REALLY** LIKES ME...I GET JUST AS DEPRESSED AS I ALWAYS DID..

**Panel 3:** POOR CHARLIE BROWN..

**Panel 4:** OF ALL THE CHARLIE BROWNS IN THIS WORLD HE'S THE CHARLIE BROWNEST!

**Panel 1:** IF I TELL YOU SOMETHING, LUCY, WILL YOU PROMISE NOT TO LAUGH? / I PROMISE

**Panel 2:** THIS IS VERY PERSONAL, AND I DON'T WANT YOU TO LAUGH. / YOU HAVE MY SOLEMN PROMISE.

**Panel 3:** SOMETIMES I LIE AWAKE AT NIGHT LISTENING FOR A VOICE THAT WILL CRY, "WE LIKE YOU, CHARLIE BROWNNNN!"

**Panel 4:** HA HA HA HA

DOES IT BOTHER YOU KNOWING THAT NOBODY LIKES YOU, CHARLIE BROWN?

OF COURSE, IT BOTHERS ME! WOULDN'T IT BOTHER YOU IF YOU KNEW NOBODY LIKED YOU?

I DON'T THINK SO... I DON'T CARE IF ANYBODY LIKES ME OR NOT...

JUST SO I'M POPULAR!

---

English Essay: "What I Did This Summer"

I played ball, and I went to camp.

ONE, TWO, THREE, FOUR, FIVE, SIX, SEVEN, EIGHT....

NINE HUNDRED AND NINETY-TWO WORDS TO GO!

NEXT YEAR I'M GOING TO BE A CHANGED PERSON! / THAT'S A LAUGH, CHARLIE BROWN

I MEAN IT! I'M GOING TO BE STRONG AND FIRM... / FORGET IT..YOU'LL ALWAYS BE WISHY-WASHY!

WHY CAN'T I CHANGE JUST A LITTLE BIT?

I'LL BE WISHY ONE DAY AND WASHY THE NEXT!

I once read a newspaper article that labelled Charlie Brown "a loser". That never occured to me. A real loser would stop trying. Comedy has always revolved around characters who are "losers". Look at Charlie Chaplin or Laurel and Hardy.

In the beginning of the strip Charlie Brown used to be a little more flippant, but then he fell into place. I like Charlie Brown for his kindness and gentleness. He's certainly the only character who's all one thing. He's a caricature. We all know what it's like to lose, but Charlie Brown keeps losing outrageously. It's not that he's a loser: he's really a decent little sort. But nothing seems to work out right. I used to say he tried too hard and that he wanted everyone to like him too much, but I've grown away from that.

THAT LITTLE RED HAIRED GIRL IS AT THE DOOR...

SHE SAYS SHE FORGOT TO GIVE YOU A VALENTINE SO SHE CAME BY TO GIVE IT TO YOU NOW...

APRIL FOOL!!

..OR FEBRUARY OR MARCH OR WHATEVER

SOMETIMES I LIE AWAKE AT NIGHT, AND I ASK MYSELF, "IS THIS ALL THERE IS?"

THEN I HEAR A VOICE THAT SAYS..

"WHAT KIND OF A QUESTION IS THAT?"

HI! MY NAME IS EMILY..WOULD YOU LIKE TO BE MY DANCE PARTNER?

WELL, SURE.. BUT I'M NOT VERY GOOD..

IT'LL BE EASY.. "SLOW, SLOW, QUICK, QUICK"

HOW ABOUT, "SLOW, SLOW, PANIC, PANIC"?

ASK YOUR DAD IF HE WANTS ME TO RAKE YOUR LEAVES..

OUR LEAVES ARE STILL ON THE TREES..

YOU'RE RIGHT..

SHOULD I COME BACK TOMORROW?

I have always been fond of the old sayings that the previous generation laid on us. "You never miss the water 'til the well runs dry" was something I heard my mother say many times, and whenever we would return home in the evening, as we pulled into the driveway, she invariably would say, "Home again, Finnegan!" My Aunt Marian had a motto, "Never marry a trumpet player," which, of course, she eventually did. My favourite was my grandmother's: "When your children are young, they step on your toes. When they grow up, they step on your heart."

Favorite Quotations

"a lopsided man runs fastest along the little side-hills of success."

WHO SAID THAT, MOSES?

NO, A MAN NAMED FRANK MOORE COLBY...

IT SOUNDS LIKE SOMETHING MOSES WOULD HAVE SAID...

ACTUALLY, IT DOESN'T SOUND AT ALL LIKE SOMETHING MOSES WOULD HAVE SAID!

HOW DO YOU KNOW? YOU NEVER TALKED TO MOSES, DID YOU?

MOSES LIKED TO SAY THINGS LIKE THAT!

IF MOSES HAD THOUGHT OF IT, MOSES WOULD HAVE SAID IT!

BAM!
BAM!
BAM!

IS IT SUPPERTIME ALREADY?

I'M SORRY...YOU MAY NOT BELIEVE THIS, BUT I WAS READING THE BOOK OF PSALMS, AND FORGOT WHAT TIME IT WAS...

WHAT ARE YOU DOING?

NOW WHAT?

PSALM FIFTY... VERSE TWELVE..."IF I WERE HUNGRY, I WOULD NOT TELL THEE"

GIVE ME TWO WEEKS, AND I'LL FIND A VERSE TO ANSWER YOU!

I have underlined words and sentences in one of the Bibles that has always been my study Bible, but when I look at those words and sentences now, I can't remember why they were underlined. One day I was re-reading a short story by Joanne Greenberg, and I came across a long passage that I had marked off, but as I looked at it, I couldn't remember why. Perhaps I had meant to ask her about it the next time we talked on the phone, but now I have no idea what it could be that I wanted to ask her. My Revised Standard version of the Bible is filled with markings, for I have gone through it word for word with study groups at least four times and, of course, I have used it on various occasions to begin speeches. I know that the underlined passages served some purpose, but here and there are verses that have no special meaning to me. It is almost as if a friend had secretly opened the book and made some markings just to tease me. What was the spirit trying to say to me then that I no longer need to hear? Or, what was I listening for then that I no longer care about?

---

---

---

OH, NO! DON'T TELL ME! NOT AGAIN!

HERE'S YOUR PIECE FOR THE CHRISTMAS PROGRAM..

"SO THE WORDS SPOKEN THROUGH JEREMIAH THE PROPHET WERE FULFILLED: 'A VOICE WAS HEARD IN RAMA, WAILING AND LOUD LAMENTS; IT WAS RACHEL WEEPING FOR HER CHILDREN, AND REFUSING ALL CONSOLATION BECAUSE THEY WERE NO MORE.'" GOOD GRIEF !!

MEMORIZE IT, AND BE READY TO RECITE IT BY NEXT SUNDAY!

I CAN'T MEMORIZE SOMETHING LIKE THIS IN A **WEEK**! THIS IS GOING TO TAKE **RESEARCH**!

WHO WAS JEREMIAH? WHERE WAS RAMA? WHY WAS RACHEL SO UPSET?

YOU CAN'T RECITE SOMETHING UNTIL YOU KNOW THE "WHO," THE "WHERE" AND THE "WHY"!

I'LL TELL YOU THE "WHO," THE "WHERE" AND THE "WHY"!

YOU START MEMORIZING RIGHT NOW, OR YOU'LL KNOW **WHO** IS GOING TO SLUG YOU, AND YOU'LL KNOW **WHERE** SHE'S GOING TO SLUG YOU AND YOU'LL KNOW **WHY** SHE SLUGGED YOU !!!

CHRISTMAS IS NOT ONLY GETTING TOO COMMERCIAL, IT'S GETTING TOO DANGEROUS!

In recent years, we have hosted a professional senior tennis tournament at the Ice Arena in Santa Rosa with such stars as Billie Jean King, Rosie Casals, and Virginia Wade. The tournament is called The Women's Tennis Classic, and the winner's trophy the Snoopy Cup. One year Kerry Ried flew in from Hilton Head to join the group, and on her first night in California, she phoned home to talk to her husband and two little girls. The three-year-old said, "Good luck, Mommy. . . . Bring home the Smurf Cup."

HEY, PARTNER, IT'S ME, MOLLY VOLLEY!

?

THERE'S A MIXED DOUBLES TENNIS TOURNAMENT THIS WEEK... I HOPE YOU'RE IN GOOD SHAPE...

I KNOW I'VE GAINED WEIGHT, BUT IF YOU SAY ANYTHING, I'LL HIT YOU OVER THE HEAD WITH MY RACKET!

WHEN I KNOW I COULD GET HIT OVER THE HEAD WITH A RACKET, I CAN BE THE SOUL OF DISCRETION!

---

LOOK AT HER .. I'LL BET SHE'S GAINED THIRTY POUNDS...

WHY DO I ALWAYS GET FAT PARTNERS?

HEY, PARTNER, I HOPE YOU'RE NOT THINKING ABOUT HOW FAT I AM!

WHY WOULD I THINK THAT?

---

HERE, PARTNER, LET'S SEE YOU HIT A FEW SERVES...

YOUR HANDS LOOK KIND OF SMALL, AND YOU DON'T HAVE ANY POCKETS...

HOW'RE YOU GONNA HOLD TWO BALLS WHEN YOU SERVE?

---

LOOK WHO WE PLAY IN THE FIRST ROUND... "CRYBABY" BOOBIE AND "BAD CALL" BENNY!

BOOBIE COMPLAINS ABOUT EVERYTHING, AND BENNY CALLS EVERYTHING "OUT"!

I REMEMBER THE LAST TIME I PLAYED AGAINST HIM...

AS SOON AS I OPENED THE CAN OF BALLS, HE CALLED THEM "OUT"!

WE'RE PLAYING AGAINST A **DOG**? | IT'S A MIXED DOUBLES TOURNAMENT, ISN'T IT?

I'LL HAVE YOU KNOW HE WAS THE NUMBER ONE PLAYER AT THE DAISY HILL PUPPY FARM...

THAT'S RIGHT, ISN'T IT, SNOOPY?

ACTUALLY, I LOST A TIEBREAKER IN THE FINALS TO A LEFT-HANDED SAINT BERNARD!

WHAT'S GOING ON? | IT'S THE FIRST ROUND OF THE MIXED DOUBLES TENNIS TOURNAMENT

SNOOPY AND MOLLY VOLLEY ARE PLAYING "CRYBABY" BOOBIE AND "BAD CALL" BENNY!

SEE? THEY'RE JUST INTRODUCING THEMSELVES NOW..I IMAGINE THEY'RE BEING VERY POLITE...

WELL, IF IT ISN'T "FAT LEGS" VOLLEY!!

I CAN'T BELIEVE IT! MOLLY VOLLEY HIT "BAD CALL" BENNY IN THE MOUTH!

NOBODY CALLS ME "FAT LEGS," KID!!

YOU HIT MY PARTNER IN THE MOUTH! | SHUT UP, "CRYBABY"!

OH, TO BE AT WIMBLEDON NOW THAT SPRING IS HERE...

In 1974 I was invited by Mr. Ed Wilson, president of that year's Tournament of Roses Parade in Pasadena, to be the grand marshal. On the day before the parade, we were guests at a very large luncheon. A band was playing as we entered the hall, and the conductor asked me what my favourite number was. I must have been overwhelmed by the grandness of the occasion, because not understanding the question, I said, "two."

THE SECOND PROBLEM, MA'AM? YES, MA'AM...

AT THE BLACKBOARD... IN FRONT OF THE WHOLE CLASS...SECOND PROBLEM...

FOR THE FIRST TIME IN MY LIFE, I BELIEVE IN SCHOOL PRAYER!

---

I HATE SCHOOL...ALL THEY DO IS CRITICIZE US...

I QUOTE, SIR, FROM THE THIRTEENTH CHAPTER OF THE "BOOK OF PROVERBS"

"IF YOU REFUSE CRITICISM, YOU WILL END IN POVERTY AND DISGRACE..IF YOU ACCEPT CRITICISM, YOU ARE ON THE ROAD TO FAME"

THROW ME THOSE "D MINUSES," MA'AM.. I'M ON MY WAY TO HOLLYWOOD!

THE ANSWER IS 'TWELVE'!

IT IS?

HOW ABOUT THAT!

DRINKS ARE ON ME!

**YOU LOOK LIKE YOU'RE SINKING, SIR...** **I AM, MARCIE**

**I'M DROWNING IN A SEA OF UNANSWERED QUESTIONS...**

**NOW, I SUDDENLY SURFACE! I SPLASH FRANTICALLY... "HELP!" I CRY..."SAVE ME!"**

**NOW, I SINK FOR THE SECOND TIME...QUESTIONS POUR OVER MY HEAD..."WHO WAS VOLTAIRE?" "WHO WAS CATO THE ELDER?"**

**NOW, I COME UP FOR THE LAST TIME... SPUTTERING HALF-ANSWERS..SPITTING OUT VERBS, INFINITIVES, COMMAS...**

**I SINK BENEATH THE SURFACE.. I'M GONE, MARCIE... I'M GONE...**

**MARK THE SPOT WHERE YOU LAST SAW ME..MARK THE SPOT WHERE I DROWNED IN A SEA OF "D MINUSES" AND "INCOMPLETES"**

**ANOTHER SCHOLAR CAUGHT IN THE UNDERTOW, MA'AM**

Some time in the early part of 1980, I received a phone call from attorney Stephen Trattner of Washington, D.C. He told me that he represented Skippy, Inc., the "successor-in-interest and owner of federal and common law trademarks in the term SKIPPY, emanating from the *Skippy* cartoon and comic strip created by Percy L. Crosby in 1923." His client was suing CPC International, Inc., for illegal use of the name "Skippy" on their peanut butter product. He asked if I would be willing to be an "expert witness" in the trial. At first, I was very doubtful of his chances, even though I was certain in my own mind that the theft of the famous cartoon name was obvious. He explained several points of law, however, that easily persuaded me at least to submit to a deposition, and he added that Mr. Milton Caniff, famous creator of *Terry and the Pirates* and *Steve Canyon*, had also agreed to be an expert witness.

The deposition was interesting because I felt able to counter any suggestions that the label on the peanut butter jars did not really reflect Percy Crosby's style. I was able, I felt, to explain how a simple drawing of a board fence with heavy brush stroke lettering was easily identified and had been as much a part of *Skippy* as Snoopy's doghouse is in *Peanuts*, and that these symbols, when used over and over, actually help to promote creativity and produce ideas. At one point in the questioning, I was asked by attorney Joanne Alper, "Is it your testimony that Crosby had exclusive rights to the use of a fence in a comic strip?"

"No," I replied. "If I were to create a label, knowing that I could not use the *Skippy* character itself, and wanted to use the name 'Skippy' and pick an element that people would recognize and know that this was related to the *Skippy* comic strip, I would have picked one of two things. I would have drawn the homemade go-cart that they always had and lettered 'Skippy' on the side, knowing that people would immediately say that was Skippy's go-cart; or, I would have used one of his typical wooden fences and used his style of lettering."

What I was trying to get into the record was my opinion of how an advertising agency might borrow some valuable elements from a successful cartoon that would be recognized by everyone without actually using the main character. I also was anxious to further Stephen Trattner's contention that the use of the fence and the lettering was just as much a theft as the use of Skippy's face would have been. I thought I had made some good points, and was ready for the trial, wondering, too, what sort of deposition Milt had given. Milt Caniff is one of the most remarkable men in the history of cartooning. I have seen him in meetings where he has sat, appearing almost not to be listening at all, but then rising to make a point that was swift, sure, and sensible. Stephen Trattner met Jeannie, Milt, and me at Dulles Airport in August, and on our way into the city, we discussed the issues of the trial, and Milt remarked, "We've got to show them that we've come to play hard ball!" I was confident that I had a good partner.

That evening, we attended a dinner at a beautiful country club where we met various relatives of Joan Crosby Tibbetts and the attorneys. Confidence was everywhere as we all agreed to the righteousness of our cause; Milt and I especially, feeling that we were doing something for the memory of Percy Crosby and for the comic industry itself. We were about to right a terrible wrong. My wife, Jeannie, recalled that at one point, attorney Trattner asked her, "What do you think is the most important point I should try to get across?" She was caught up in the enthusiasm of the guests at the dinner and told Stephen that he should try to bring out the tragic history of Percy Crosby's incarceration in the mental ward of King's Park Veterans' Hospital on Long Island for sixteen years, where he eventually died. He should try to convince the judge that Crosby's inability to communicate from his imprisonment caused the time-delay in bringing any action to stop the use of the *Skippy* name. He should try to convince the judge that justice should be done, even though, legally, the statute of limitations had apparently expired. Much to her embarrassment, the next day at the trial, the judge wouldn't even listen to this story, and said, "We know all this. We don't have to listen to this. Get on with the case." Jeannie thought to herself, "I should have kept my mouth shut."

Stephen Trattner was late meeting us for breakfast the next day, the trial day, because he said he had been making some last minute additions to his opening statement. We left our hotel to walk the short distance to the courthouse. After walking three blocks, Stephen said, "I think we're going in the wrong direction!" This statement, revealing his obvious nervousness, amused me and later prompted a Snoopy cartoon.

The courtroom had a lot more people in it than we had expected, and Judge Oren Lewis apparently was as surprised, for his first words were,

"What are all these people doing here? I hope they're not all witnesses!" Judge Lewis, I was told, was frequently referred to as "Roarin' Oren," and his actions could terrify attorneys. We could see this immediately as Joanne Alper, representing CPC International, Inc., began her opening statements. It did my heart good to see her suffer the remarks of the judge, for I considered her behaviour to Stephen during my deposition as unnecessarily rude. Judge Lewis continually interrupted both attorneys, finally demanding that "he didn't have to hear all of this," that the case really was "cut and dried," and "let's hear a witness. Get on with the case." Milt Caniff was called to the stand, asked to identify himself, etc., and then, without being given the opportunity to testify to anything, was dismissed. It was disappointing and actually degrading. It taught me, however, that as I was called to take the oath, not to say anything beyond "Yes, sir" and "No, sir." I had one very brief skirmish with the opposing attorney as she tried to have me admit that "Skippy" was not necessarily a unique or original name. Shortly thereafter, we were dismissed, and found ourselves out in the hall grumbling about the ridiculousness of the whole episode, and questioning the tenure of federal court justices.

Joan Crosby Tibbetts thanked us for coming all the way across the country to try to help, especially at our own expense. I told her that if she really wanted to thank me in a material way, I would love to have an original *Skippy* Sunday page, and she agreed to send me one.

The following April, I received a letter from Attorney Stephen Trattner, informing me that Judge Lewis ruled against them, but that he was filing an appeal. I have heard nothing more from him, although we do exchange Christmas cards, and I have never received the original *Skippy* Sunday page.

**Strip 1**

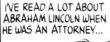
I'VE READ A LOT ABOUT ABRAHAM LINCOLN WHEN HE WAS AN ATTORNEY...

NOT ONCE, ON THE DAY OF A TRIAL, WAS HE UNABLE TO FIND THE COURTHOUSE

LIFE WAS SIMPLER THEN!

**Strip 2**

YES, MA'AM..HE'S AN ATTORNEY

HE WANTS TO ORDER AN 8½-INCH X 11¾-INCH CANARY YELLOW, FIFTY PAGE LEGAL PAD...

ANYTHING ELSE?

HE WANTS TO KNOW IF YOU HAVE ANYONE YOU WANT SUED...

**Strip 3**

WHEN ABRAHAM LINCOLN WAS AN ATTORNEY, HE WOULD ARRIVE AT HIS OFFICE AT NINE O'CLOCK

HE WOULD IMMEDIATELY STRETCH OUT ON THE COUCH, AND MUCH TO HIS PARTNER'S ANNOYANCE, BEGIN TO READ THE NEWSPAPERS OUT LOUD

I'LL HAVE TO REMEMBER THAT

THE SECRET TO BEING A GOOD ATTORNEY IS TO ANNOY YOUR PARTNER

HERE'S THE WORLD FAMOUS ATTORNEY ON HIS WAY TO THE COURTHOUSE...

"AN UNINTENTIONAL MISTAKE ABOUT WHAT THE TRUE FACTS ARE IS A 'MISTAKE OF FACT'"

THEN I WAS RIGHT..

LUNCH IS AT ONE-THIRTY!

---

HERE'S THE WORLD FAMOUS ATTORNEY ON HIS WAY TO THE COURTHOUSE...

THIS IS A MAXIM OF JURISPRUDENCE..."A THING CONTINUES TO EXIST AS LONG AS IS USUAL WITH THINGS OF THIS NATURE"

DID YOU UNDERSTAND THAT?

I DIDN'T EVEN UNDERSTAND THE LUNCH MENU!

---

HERE'S THE WORLD FAMOUS LAWYER ON HIS WAY TO THE COURTHOUSE

WHEN LAWYERS SAY, "SINE MORA," THEY MEAN, "WITHOUT DELAY"

LAWYERS SAY A LOT OF THINGS

---

THE COURT WILL NOT AID THOSE WHO HAVE COMMITTED ILLEGAL ACTS IN A MATTER...

..AND THEN ASK THE COURT'S HELP TO RECOVER FOR ANY INJURY THEY MAY HAVE SUFFERED AS A RESULT THEREOF!

RATS!

HERE'S THE WORLD FAMOUS ATTORNEY ON HIS WAY TO THE TRIAL...

IF YOU'RE GOING TO COURT, YOU SHOULD REMEMBER THIS...

"THAT WHICH OUGHT TO HAVE BEEN DONE IS TO BE REGARDED AS DONE, IN FAVOR OF HIM IN WHOM, AND AGAINST HIM FROM WHOM, PERFORMANCE IS DUE!"

THAT WON'T EVEN FIT IN MY BRIEFCASE!

---

LAW AND LAWYERS ARE ALWAYS WITH US

WE ALL HAVE TO DEAL WITH THE LAW FROM THE VERY DAY WE'RE BORN

THAT'S TRUE

JUST LAST WEEK I SUED A BABY!

"A MISDEMEANOR IS A MINOR OFFENSE"

LIKE MAYBE JAYWALKING

"A FELONY IS A MORE SERIOUS CRIME"

LIKE NOT FEEDING THE DOG!

I think one of the worst traits that a person can have is to possess sensitive areas that make others uncomfortable. No one can relax around someone who is so sensitive about his religious, political, or other beliefs that they have to watch everything they say.

CLOUDS ARE FASCINATING

SOME CLOUDS ARE ABSOLUTELY BEAUTIFUL...

SOME CLOUDS ARE UGLY..

...AND VERY SENSITIVE!

---

WHAT AM I DOING? I'M ADDRESSING CHRISTMAS CARDS!

AREN'T THEY CUTE?

EACH ONE HAS A LITTLE BUNNY ON IT DRESSED UP LIKE A SHEPHERD...

DON'T SAY I'M NOT RELIGIOUS!!

I WAS PRAYING FOR GREATER PATIENCE AND UNDERSTANDING, BUT I QUIT...

I WAS AFRAID I MIGHT GET IT

**S L A M**

GOOD MORNING

GET LOST, KID!

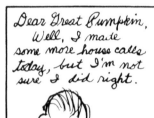

*Dear Great Pumpkin, Well, I made some more house calls today, but I'm not sure I did right.*

GOOD MORNING, MY NAME IS LINUS VAN PELT, AND I'M HERE TO TELL YOU ABOUT "THE GREAT PUMPKIN"

THE GREAT WHO?

THE GREAT PUMPKIN RISES OUT OF THE PUMPKIN PATCH ON HALLOWEEN NIGHT, AND BRINGS TOYS TO ALL THE GOOD LITTLE CHILDREN IN THE WORLD...

NOW, I HAVE SOME LITERATURE HERE THAT I CAN LEAVE WITH YOU, AND..

I'M SORRY, WE HAVE OUR OWN CHURCH

I DIDN'T SAY ANYTHING ABOUT CHURCH!

*So then I tried to explain that you are non-denominational. Did I do right?*

STUPID!

FOOLISH, THAT'S WHAT IT IS! STUPID AND FOOLISH!

DEAR GREAT PUMPKIN, HALLOWEEN WILL SOON BE HERE. WE ARE ALL LOOKING FORWARD TO YOUR ARRIVAL.

RIDICULOUS!

NEXT WEEK YOU WILL RISE OUT OF THE PUMPKIN PATCH, AND FLY THROUGH THE AIR.

ABSURD!

YOU WILL BRING PRESENTS TO ALL THE GOOD LITTLE BOYS AND GIRLS IN THE WORLD.

PREPOSTEROUS!

I HAVE TRIED TO BE GOOD ALL YEAR LONG, AND HOPE THAT YOU WILL BRING ME LOTS OF PRESENTS.

CRAZY! COMPLETELY CRAZY!

OUTRAGEOUS!

INSANE! TOTALLY AND COMPLETELY INSANE!

PLUNK!

DID YOU TELL HIM I'VE TRIED TO BE GOOD TOO?!

SCHULZ

OW!

I GOT A SLIVER!

WHAT'S THE MATTER WITH YOU?

I HAVE A SLIVER IN MY FINGER..

AH, HA! THAT MEANS YOU'RE BEING PUNISHED FOR SOMETHING!

WHAT HAVE YOU DONE WRONG LATELY?

I HAVEN'T DONE ANYTHING WRONG!

YOU HAVE A SLIVER, HAVEN'T YOU? THAT'S A MISFORTUNE, ISN'T IT? YOU'RE BEING PUNISHED WITH MISFORTUNE BECAUSE YOU'VE BEEN BAD!

NOW, WAIT A MINUTE.. DOES..

WHAT DO YOU KNOW ABOUT IT, CHARLIE BROWN? THIS IS A SIGN! THIS IS A DIRECT SIGN OF PUNISHMENT! LINUS HAS DONE SOMETHING VERY WRONG, AND NOW HE HAS TO SUFFER MISFORTUNE!

I KNOW ALL ABOUT THESE THINGS! I KNOW THAT A...

IT'S OUT! IT JUST POPPED RIGHT OUT!

THUS ENDETH THE THEOLOGICAL LESSON FOR TODAY!

There must be different kinds of loneliness, or at least different degrees of loneliness, but the most terrifying loneliness is not experienced by everyone and can be understood by only a few. I compare the panic in this kind of loneliness to the dog we see running frantically down the road pursuing the family car. He is not really being left behind, for the family knows it is to return, but for that moment in his limited understanding, he is being left alone forever, and he has to run and run to survive. It is no wonder that we make terrible choices in our lives to avoid loneliness.

**Row 1:**
- SO HERE I AM AT CAMP, LYING IN MY BUNK
- I HOPE NO QUEEN SNAKES CRAWL IN HERE DURING THE NIGHT...
- WHAT IF MY MOTHER AND DAD MOVE AWAY WHILE I'M GONE, AND DON'T TELL ME?

---

**Row 2:**
- "PET COLUMN" AIREDALES, BOXERS, GOLDEN RETRIEVERS...
- GREAT DANES, IRISH SETTERS, LABS...
- NO BEAGLES... GOOD!
- IT'S ALWAYS NICE TO KNOW THEY'RE NOT SELLING YOU BEHIND YOUR BACK

---

**Row 3:**
- I KNOW YOU LOVE YOUR PIANO MORE THAN YOU LOVE ME
- I CAN LIVE WITH THAT
- WHO KNOWS? MAYBE SOMEDAY THINGS WILL CHANGE
- I'M HAPPY JUST BEING IN THE "ON DECK CIRCLE"

---

**Row 4:**
- WHY DO WE ALWAYS TEACH LITTLE KIDS TO WAVE "BYE-BYE"?
- BECAUSE FOR THE REST OF HIS LIFE PEOPLE WILL BE LEAVING HIM
- HELLO, THERE!

I always enjoy drawing the episodes where Marcie and Peppermint Patty are attending a "Tiny Tots" concert. They always complain that each time they go, the orchestra plays "Peter and the Wolf" and I am certain that there is a lot of truth in this.

Some time in the sixties, I was approached by the conductor of the San Francisco Youth Symphony to perform "Peter and the Wolf" with them. I warned him that I know nothing about music, and even though I would be reading the narrative, I probably would have no idea when to speak and when to remain silent. He assured me that there would be no problem because he would be right next to me on the stage and could easily cue me. He even offered to go over the score with me, but soon found this to be useless because I could not read music. He left me with a recording of the work as recited by Peter Ustinov. This saved me, for I listened to the recording at least fifty times, and made my own crude notes such as "the violins go zip, zip, zip," and on the day of the perform-ance made only one very slight miscue.

All in all it was a great triumph for one who still sits in awe at sym-phony concerts watching musicians perform. I am not sure, however, that all of the music played at these "Tiny Tots" concerts is as inspiring to these little ones as the committees who arrange the programmes would like to think they are. I saw a concert on television one day, and when the camera panned through the audience, each child's face seemed to indi-cate that he or she just might prefer to be somewhere else.

Row R.. Seat 3

THESE ARE GOOD SEATS

I SEE THEY'RE PLAYING "PETER AND THE WOLF" AGAIN...EVERY TIME WE GO TO A "TINY TOTS" CONCERT, THEY PLAY "PETER AND THE WOLF"!

WHERE'S YOUR TICKET STUB, MARCIE?

I THREW IT AWAY

YOU SHOULD ALWAYS SAVE YOUR TICKET STUB, MARCIE

I DON'T NEED IT..I'M ALREADY IN MY SEAT...

I ALWAYS SAVE MY TICKET STUB IN CASE THEY HAVE A DRAWING FOR A BIG PRIZE...

AT A CONCERT?

I'M THINKING MAYBE THEY'LL GIVE AWAY A VIOLIN..THEY SEEM TO HAVE MORE THAN THEY NEED..

YOU'RE WEIRD, SIR!

In 1978, I was informed by Monsieur Robert LePalme of the International Pavilion of Humor of Montreal, Canada, that I had been selected as International Cartoonist of the Year. He invited me to attend the judging of their yearly cartoon contest, and to be the honorary chairman of the judging committee. On the first evening, my wife, Jeannie, Lee Mendelson, our TV producer, and I were guests at what was to us a very nice affair. As vichyssoise was being served, Lee spoke loudly to me across the table: "Eat your soup, Sparky, before it gets cold."

"Sir," said the very proper man seated next to Lee, "it is supposed to be cold!"

Monsieur LePalme is a delightful man, short in stature, but very tall in humour and dignity. He had been very anxious for us to enjoy ourselves while we were in Montreal, but for some reason, that first dinner was to him a great disappointment. Things just were not up to his standard. Therefore, he wanted everything on the next evening to be perfect. I asked him how we should dress for this dinner.

"Should we wear ties?"

"Yes, we should wear ties."

"Why?" I asked. "Who is going to be there?"

"We shall dress for ourselves," said LePalme.

When we got to the restaurant, LePalme told the owner that he was placing us in his hands, and to serve us whatever he thought we might like. The dinner, of course, was excellent, and the wines were as special as LePalme hoped they would be, although I certainly couldn't tell, being as ignorant of wine as it is possible to be. Along about eleven o'clock, I noticed that I had accumulated a row of glasses in front of me that was quite impressive; a water glass, two red wines (untouched), two white wines (only slightly touched), and a Seven-Up. Robert LePalme looked at this row of glasses, leaned over to me and asked, "May I say something to you?"

"Yes, Robert. What is it?"

"I do not wish to offend."

"That's all right, Robert, a little offending never hurt anybody."

"You," he said, "are the most simple man I have ever met."

SUPPERTIME!

SUPPERTIME!

OH, IT'S SUPPERTIME! IT'S SUPPERTIME!!!

YAHOO! IT'S SUPPERTIME!

SUPPERTIME! SUPPERTIME! SUPPERTIME! GOOD OL' SUP, SUP, SUP, SUPPERTIME!

SUPPERTIME!

I MUST ADMIT HE'S A VERY SATISFYING PERSON TO COOK FOR

A high school student wrote to me once as part of a class project, asking me if I would name my three heroes. I answered, "General Eisenhower, Billie Jean King, and Sam Snead." I have often wondered what the teacher's reaction was.

OLGA KORBUT HAS BEEN BUGGING ME FOR LESSONS!

---

MARCIE, HELP ME PICK OUT A LIBRARY BOOK

MAYBE SOMETHING ABOUT PATTY BERG...SHE'S ONE OF MY IDOLS...

MOSES WARNED US ABOUT WORSHIPPING IDOLS, SIR...

MOSES NEVER SAW PATTY BERG HIT A SEVEN-IRON!

---

WHAT ARE YOU DOING?

I'M TRYING TO COME UP WITH SOME KIND OF ITEM I CAN SELL DURING THE BICENTENNIAL, AND MAKE A MILLION DOLLARS...

HOW DOES THIS LOOK? IT'S A DRAWING OF GEORGE WASHINGTON, BETSY ROSS, HARRY TRUMAN AND BILLIE JEAN KING PLAYING MIXED DOUBLES!

THAT'S PATRIOTIC, ISN'T IT?

HARRY AND BILLIE JEAN WOULD TAKE 'EM IN STRAIGHT SETS!

---

THERE'S THE HOUSE WHERE THAT LITTLE RED-HAIRED GIRL LIVES...

MAYBE SHE'LL SEE ME, AND COME RUSHING OUT TO THANK ME FOR THE CHRISTMAS CARD I SENT HER...MAYBE SHE'LL EVEN GIVE ME A HUG...

MAYBE BILLIE JEAN KING WILL CALL ME TONIGHT, AND INVITE ME OUT TO DINNER

"JOHNNY MILLER ALL THE WAY"

"...FOUR TO THREE IN TEN INNINGS"

"AND THAT'S SPORTS FOR TONIGHT"

THAT'S SPORTS ?!! WHAT DO YOU MEAN, THAT'S SPORTS ?!!

ALL YOU TOLD US ABOUT WERE MEN! WHAT ABOUT WOMEN IN SPORTS ?!!!

YOU DIDN'T SAY ANYTHING ABOUT JOANNE CARNER, OR SALLY LITTLE, OR HOLLIS STACY, OR BILLIE JEAN KING, OR ROSIE CASALS OR SHARON WALSH! AND WHAT ABOUT DONNA ADAMEK, BETH HEIDEN OR MARY DECKER ?

DID YOU TELL US WHAT CONNI PLACE HAS BEEN DOING? AND HOW ABOUT ALISON ROWE, AND TRACY CAULKINS, AND KAREN ROGERS, AND EVELYN ASHFORD, AND ANN MEYERS, AND JUDY SLADKY AND SARAH DOCTER ?!

DID YOU SAY ANYTHING ABOUT JENNIFER HARDING OR SHIRLEY MULDOWNEY? WHAT DO YOU MEAN, "THAT'S SPORTS" ?!!

WHAT DO YOU WANT TO WATCH NEXT, SIR? THERE'RE SOME OLD MOVIES ON THE OTHER CHANNELS..

"THE MEN," "A MAN FOR ALL SEASONS" AND "ALL THE KING'S MEN"

I CAN'T STAND IT...

BEETHOVEN... HA!

EVERYONE TALKS ABOUT HOW GREAT BEETHOVEN WAS...

BEETHOVEN WASN'T SO GREAT!

WHAT DO YOU MEAN, BEETHOVEN WASN'T SO GREAT?

HE NEVER GOT HIS PICTURE ON BUBBLE GUM CARDS, DID HE?

HAVE YOU EVER SEEN HIS PICTURE ON BUBBLE GUM CARDS? HUH?

HOW CAN YOU SAY SOMEONE IS GREAT WHO'S NEVER HAD HIS PICTURE ON BUBBLE GUM CARDS?

THAT'S WHAT I MEAN WHEN I SAY BEETHOVEN WASN'T SO GREAT!

THIS HAS BEEN A GOOD DAY!

SCHULZ

When you're a professional, creativity should not require certain moods, although I will admit that moods of despair or even loneliness seem, strangely enough, to produce good humour. If you are a person who looks at the funny side of things, then sometimes when you are the lowest, when everything seems totally hopeless, you will come up with some of your best ideas.

Happiness does not create humour. There's nothing funny about being happy. Sadness creates humour. Krazy Kat getting hit on the head by a brick from Ignatz Mouse is funny. All the sad things that happen to Charlie Chaplin are funny. It's funny because it's not happening to us.

I'M IN SAD SHAPE..

GOOD MORNING SIR.. SIT RIGHT DOWN..

FINE... I WAS AFRAID I MIGHT NEED AN APPOINTMENT..

THE DOCTOR IS IN

PSYCHIATRIC HELP 5¢

THE DOCTOR IS IN

WHAT CAN YOU DO WHEN YOU DON'T FIT IN?

WHAT CAN YOU DO WHEN LIFE SEEMS TO BE PASSING YOU BY?

THE DOCTOR

FOLLOW ME..I WANT TO SHOW YOU SOMETHING..

SEE THE HORIZON OVER THERE? SEE HOW BIG THIS WORLD IS? SEE HOW MUCH ROOM THERE IS FOR EVERYBODY?

HAVE YOU EVER SEEN ANY OTHER WORLDS?

NO

AS FAR AS YOU KNOW THIS IS THE ONLY WORLD THERE IS.... RIGHT?

RIGHT

THERE ARE NO OTHER WORLDS FOR YOU TO LIVE IN...RIGHT?

RIGHT

YOU WERE BORN TO LIVE IN THIS WORLD...RIGHT?

RIGHT

WELL, LIVE IN IT, THEN!

FIVE CENTS, PLEASE..

SCHULZ

WAAH!

STOP CRYING, RERUN... HAVE A COOKIE

JUST REMEMBER THIS... THE DAY IS COMING WHEN A COOKIE WON'T SOLVE ALL YOUR PROBLEMS

UNTIL THEN!

---

I HATE EVERYTHING! I HATE THE WHOLE WORLD!

I THOUGHT YOU HAD INNER PEACE

I DO

BUT I STILL HAVE OUTER OBNOXIOUSNESS!

THIS HAS BEEN A GOOD DAY...I HAVEN'T DONE A SINGLE THING THAT WAS STUPID...

HAVE YOU DONE ANYTHING THAT WAS SMART?

No.1
CRAB

SLAM!

BOY, DO I FEEL CRABBY!

MAYBE I CAN BE OF HELP

WHY DON'T YOU JUST TAKE MY PLACE HERE IN FRONT OF THE TV WHILE I GO AND FIX YOU A NICE SNACK?

SOMETIMES WE ALL NEED A LITTLE PAMPERING TO HELP US FEEL BETTER...

SEE? I CAME RIGHT BACK! HERE'S A NICE SANDWICH FOR YOU, SOME CHOCOLATE CHIP COOKIES AND A COLD GLASS OF MILK...

NOW, IS THERE ANYTHING ELSE I CAN GET YOU?

IS THERE ANYTHING I HAVEN'T THOUGHT OF?

YES, THERE'S ONE THING THAT YOU HAVEN'T THOUGHT OF.....

I DON'T WANNA FEEL BETTER!!

OUR GENERATION HAS BEEN GIVEN THE WORKS..

ALL OF THE WORLD'S PROBLEMS ARE BEING SHOVED AT US...

WHAT DO YOU THINK WE SHOULD DO?

STICK THE NEXT GENERATION

---

CHARLIE BROWN WHAT WOULD BE YOUR REACTION IF SOMEONE SAID YOU COULD HAVE YOUR LIFE OVER AGAIN?

YOU MEAN EXACTLY AS I'VE LIVED IT? NO CHANGES? EVERYTHING HAPPENING JUST THE WAY IT DID BEFORE?

UH HUH...WHAT WOULD BE YOUR REACTION?

AAAUGHH!

I'M MAKING A LIST OF ALL THE THINGS I'VE LEARNED IN LIFE...

WELL, ACTUALLY, I'M MAKING TWO LISTS

WHY IS ONE LIST LONGER THAN THE OTHER?

THESE ARE THINGS I'VE LEARNED THE HARD WAY!

TIME OUT!

I JUST THOUGHT OF SOMETHING... TODAY IS MOTHER'S DAY...

I KNOW IT IS

WHAT DID HE SAY? I THOUGHT I HEARD SCHROEDER MENTION MOTHER'S DAY...

TODAY IS MOTHER'S DAY.. WE'RE PLAYING BASEBALL ON MOTHER'S DAY!

WE SHOULD BE HOME SERVING OUR MOTHERS BREAKFAST IN BED!

MY MOTHER IS ALWAYS DOING NICE THINGS FOR ME

EVERY TIME MY MOTHER GOES TO THE STORE SHE BRINGS ME A SURPRISE

MY MOTHER ALWAYS SINGS TO ME BEFORE I GO TO SLEEP AT NIGHT

HOW CAN WE BE SO SELFISH AS TO SPEND THIS DAY AWAY FROM HOME?

WE'RE CRUEL AND HEARTLESS!

WE HAVE NO SHAME

WE'RE NO GOOD!

WE NEVER THINK OF ANYONE BUT OURSELVES!

WAAAAAHH!!

WE'RE NO GOOD! WE'RE THOUGHTLESS! WE'RE SELFISH AND CRUEL AND...

ACTUALLY, I SENT MY MOTHER A VERY NICE CARD AND A DOZEN PINK ROSES..

On July 1, 1981, I awakened with a strange tight feeling in my chest. At first, I attributed it to having slept crooked during the night. As I dressed and then went into the kitchen, the feeling persisted, and I mentioned it to Jeannie, and a house guest. I almost turned around when driving to the studio, for the strange tightness wouldn't go away. Perhaps I'd be better off returning home. A few very deep breaths seemed to help, however, and I continued to drive. I tried to begin work, but as I sat at the drawing board, the tightness began again.

If it had not been that a very close friend of ours, Raul Diez, had gone into the hospital three days before with blood clots that travelled to his lungs, I believe I would have gone home and simply sat by the pool for the rest of the morning, dismissing the symptoms as being something that would soon pass. But, maybe what had happened to Raul was now happening to me. Dr. Lundborg's nurse said I should come in immediately, and a few quick tests convinced him to call a cardiologist who ordered me directly to the hospital. In the midst of all the tests that took up the rest of the morning, I drew a cartoon of myself lying in bed saying, "Hey, Raul, what are we doing in here?" Jeannie took it down the hall to Raul who, of course, was stunned to discover that now both of us were in trouble.

Eventually Raul struggled through several frightening crises and returned to good health. I had a two-month period where I had to decide if the four practically closed arteries that were discovered warranted by-pass surgery. It is always fascinating to look back and see what little incidents sometimes cause us to make big decisions. Jeannie and I visited Dr. Ted Folkerth, the heart surgeon, to find out once and for all just what the surgery would be like. He offered to let me see some films, but I quickly declined. My greatest fear was the knowledge that they sawed your chest open. Ted assured me that this was very simple and relatively painless. During the casual questioning and conversation, I drew out of him the story of his returning to Vietnam for a second tour of duty to learn more of surgery. It was then that I thought, "If anyone goes back to Vietnam a second time to become a better surgeon, certainly I can trust him!" Many months later, I reminded him of this. "I don't remember saying that at all," he remarked.

On the fourth night after the surgery, I lay in bed staring at the blank wall across the room. Jeannie was sitting quietly next to the bed reading the paper. When I was first admitted to the hospital, one of the nurses placed a large felt-tip pen on a cabinet and said, "Before you leave here, we want you to draw something on the wall." I am not one who goes around drawing pictures on the wall, but I felt I had to fulfill this request. It was now almost ten-thirty at night, and like all cartoon ideas, it suddenly came to me. I climbed carefully out of bed, picked up the pen and began to draw a series of five Snoopys, showing him struggling with an inhalator to make the three balls rise to the top and remain there for a moment. All patients could identify with this frustrating exercise, devised to keep the lungs clear and get them back to good working order. The last panel showed him collapsing with exhaustion and triumph.

The triumph, of course, belonged also to Jeannie and me. It was a difficult decision just to have the surgery, but now here I was standing at the wall, drawing again, exhilarated with the feeling that I had gone through something I had not been sure I was brave enough to attempt, and that maybe, somehow, drawing cartoons really was what I was meant to do.

HAVE ANY OF YOU GUYS SEEN MY BIG BROTHER?

CHARLIE BROWN? HE WASN'T FEELING WELL SO HE WENT HOME...

HE PROBABLY GOT HIT ON THE HEAD WITH TOO MANY FLY BALLS

THAT'S WHAT I SAID!

---

I SAW THE SIGN THAT SAYS "EMERGENCY ENTRANCE" SO I CAME IN...

I DON'T FEEL GOOD...I FEEL KIND OF WOOZY..

NO, MY MOM AND DAD ARE AT THE BARBERS' PICNIC SO IT WOULDN'T DO ME ANY GOOD TO GO HOME...

NO, MA'AM..I DIDN'T GET HIT ON THE HEAD WITH A FLY BALL

---

SO THIS IS WHAT IT'S LIKE TO BE IN THE EMERGENCY ROOM...

I WONDER IF I'M DYING...I WONDER IF THEY'D TELL ME IF I WERE DYING...

I WONDER IF THEY'D TELL ME IF I'M NOT DYING...MAYBE I'M ALREADY DEAD...

I WONDER IF THEY'D TELL ME

---

FIRST I WAS SURROUNDED BY DOCTORS AND NURSES.. NOW EVERYBODY'S GONE

WHAT'S HAPPENING? WHERE'D EVERYBODY GO? MAYBE I'M INCURABLE...

I GUESS I HAVE TO RELAX

JOE PATIENT

Dear Big Brother, I hope you are feeling better.

Things are fine here at home. I have moved into your room.

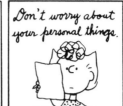
Don't worry about your personal things.

The flea market was a success.

---

I'M SO WORRIED ABOUT POOR CHARLIE BROWN LYING THERE IN THE HOSPITAL...

HE'S GOT TO GET WELL! HE'S GOT TO! OH, BOO HOO HOO HOO! SOB!

IT'S INTERESTING THAT YOU SHOULD CRY OVER HIM WHEN YOU'RE THE ONE WHO ALWAYS TREATED HIM SO MEAN!

AND STOP WIPING YOUR TEARS WITH MY PIANO!

I'M SO WORRIED ABOUT CHARLIE BROWN, I CAN'T EAT OR SLEEP...

WELL, IF YOU GET SICK, TOO, THAT SURE WON'T HELP HIM...

MAYBE IF HE THOUGHT HE WAS MAKING ME SICK, HE'D GET BETTER

MAYBE I COULD SEND HIM A THREATENING LETTER

---

---

---

IF YOU SIT ON A PARK BENCH ACROSS FROM THE HOSPITAL AND STARE UP AT HIS WINDOW, THE PATIENT GETS BETTER...

POOR CHUCK..I HATE TO THINK OF HIM LYING UP THERE IN THAT HOSPITAL ROOM

YOU KIND OF LIKE CHUCK, DON'T YOU, SIR?

WELL, I..YOU KNOW... I FEEL SORT OF..YOU KNOW...HE..I...HE..

I LOVE CHUCK! I THINK HE'S REAL NEAT!

REAL NEAT? YOU THINK HE'S REAL NEAT?

I SURE DO! SOMEDAY I HOPE HE'LL ASK ME TO THE SENIOR PROM!

IN FACT, IF HE ASKED ME, I'D EVEN MARRY CHUCK!

COME WITH ME, MARCIE

IS THIS THE EMERGENCY ENTRANCE, MA'AM? WE'RE FRIENDS OF CHARLES BROWN

I HAVE ANOTHER PATIENT FOR YOU.. I THINK SHE'S SICKER THAN HE IS!

I KEPT MY PROMISE, DIDN'T I? I DIDN'T PULL THE BALL AWAY

NO, YOU'RE RIGHT... YOU DIDN'T

BUT I MISSED THE BALL, AND KICKED YOUR HAND...I DON'T KNOW WHAT TO SAY..IS THERE ANYTHING I CAN DO?

NEXT TIME YOU GO TO THE HOSPITAL, STAY THERE!

---

YOU A DOCTOR! HA! THAT'S A BIG LAUGH!

YOU COULD NEVER BE A DOCTOR! YOU KNOW WHY?

BECAUSE YOU DON'T LOVE MANKIND, THAT'S WHY!

I LOVE MANKIND... IT'S PEOPLE I CAN'T STAND!!

THIS IS THE LAST DAY OF THE YEAR

ALL IN ALL, IT WASN'T SO BAD

YOU KNOW WHAT I LIKED ABOUT THIS YEAR?

I'M STILL IN IT!

WELL, HOW WAS THE GAME?

I HAVEN'T HAD SO MUCH FUN SINCE I HAD BYPASS SURGERY!

I don't believe that animation is superior as a medium to the comic strip any more than the novel is superior to the short story, or the stage to the movie screen. There are expanses, however, that can be attained through animation, where the simple, tiny squares of the comic strip are limiting. Our first animated half-hour specials were a direct outgrowth of the newspaper comic strips with the addition of slightly more detailed backgrounds and music being really the only difference. As we progressed to large-screen movies and more television shows, I began to grow impatient with what we were doing. I wanted to develop more emotion in our scenes and our stories.

The last movie, "Bon Voyage, Charlie Brown," showed the kids in France as exchange students. The ending was purposely open-ended in case we decided to do something else with them in Europe before their final return home. The last scene showed them bidding their recent friends good-bye, and then piling into the little French car with Snoopy driving, and heading up the road to Paris and the airport. I kept thinking how interesting it might be if they should get lost on this little trip and somehow end up at Omaha Beach and the scenes of the famous D-Day invasion of World War II. I even thought that they might pass through Belgium and we could show some landscapes affected by World War I, and how emotional it could be if one of the characters somehow could be made to recite the immortal poem "In Flanders Field."

None of this fit together in a reasonable way, however, until one night soon after my heart surgery when I was lying awake at about three o'clock in the morning. After your chest has been sawed in half, sleeping on one's back is a definite requirement for at least a few weeks, and of course sleep does not always come as easily in this restricted position. While lying there staring into the dark, I began to think some more about the story line that I wanted for this show. I knew if I could get just one phrase I could tie the whole thing together. All of a sudden the line, "What have we learned, Charlie Brown?" came to me. This helped everything else fall into place, and as soon as I got home I called Bill Melendez, the animator, and we agreed that we had something really new and different to add to television cartoon programming. The Peabody Award we received for "What Have We Learned, Charlie Brown?" was a very gratifying response to the programme, plus many wonderful letters from appreciative young viewers who said that they now understood a little better what happened on June 6, 1944. We labelled this show with the subtitle "A Tribute," because that was exactly what we wanted it to be; no more and certainly no less. It proved also that the characters of Charlie Brown, Linus, Snoopy, and the others were close enough to being real to handle delicately a subject that other animated characters would destroy.

HOLD ON TO YOUR LEG WARMERS, MARCIE! HAVE I GOT NEWS! I'VE BEEN DEPRESSED ABOUT FAILING ALL MY CLASSES, RIGHT?

SO THE SCHOOL PSYCHOLOGIST ADVISED MY DAD TO TAKE ME WITH HIM TO EUROPE THIS SUMMER! HOW ABOUT THAT?

YEARS AGO THERE USED TO BE A RADIO PROGRAM CALLED "IT PAYS TO BE IGNORANT"

JEALOUSY DOES NOT BECOME YOU, MARCIE!

---

LOOK, CHARLES... I GOT A POST CARD FROM PATTY..SHE'S IN PARIS...

Dear Marcie,
The trip over was fun. We have a nice place to stay.

I'm already doing pretty good with the language.

BONJOUR, KID!

---

Dear Chuck,
Well, your ol' friend Patty is here in Paris.

Show Snoopy this picture of me drinking root beer in a sidewalk cafe.

I REMEMBER THAT PLACE..I WAS THERE IN 1918!

---

Dear Chuck, Here is a photo of me in front of a World War II pillbox near Honfleur.

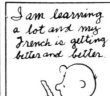

I am learning a lot and my French is getting better and better.

AU REVOIR, KID!

IT'S ADDRESSED TO BOTH OF US...

ANY PICTURES?

TWO, I THINK

Dear Marcie and Chuck,
   I am still having a good time here in Paris.

You know what we eat here for breakfast? Bread and hot chocolate!

Here is a photograph of me with a loaf of French bread.

And here is a picture of me dunking my bread in the hot chocolate.

There is a bookstore in Santa Rosa just a few blocks from the Ice Arena where I spend a lot of time, and two more blocks from the studio. I'm a virtual bookaholic—I find it very difficult to go home at night without stopping by and seeing what new things are in. There's an ice cream store right next to the bookstore, and on the front of the bookstore there's a little sign that says "No ice cream allowed," which is understandable. One day I went into the ice cream store and I said to the guy behind the counter, "It is all right if you bring books in here?" I don't think he had any idea what I was talking about.

YES, MA'AM...I READ "HANS BRINKER" ALL THE WAY THROUGH

I THOUGHT IT WAS GREAT

YOU DESERVE A LOT OF CREDIT, MA'AM...

THANK YOU FOR FORCING US TO READ IT!

*SIGH*

HAPPINESS IS HAVING YOUR OWN LIBRARY CARD!

I MAILED MY MANUSCRIPT YESTERDAY... SO WHAT HAPPENS? ZERO!

MY BOOK ISN'T IN ANY OF THE STORES OR ON A SINGLE BEST-SELLER LIST! WHAT A DISAPPOINTMENT! WHAT A BLOW!

YOU'RE THE MOST IMPATIENT AUTHOR I'VE EVER SEEN...

OH, YEAH? WELL, WHAT ABOUT MY ROYALTY STATEMENT? WHERE'S MY ROYALTY STATEMENT?

LUCY, WILL YOU READ THIS BOOK TO ME?

NO!

AW, C'MON..

NO!

PLEEEEEEZ?

"A MAN WAS BORN...HE LIVED AND HE DIED!"

"THE END!"

WHAT A FASCINATING ACCOUNT...

IT ALMOST MAKES YOU WISH YOU HAD KNOWN THE FELLOW..

I really never make appearances in classrooms because I don't feel that I am especially good at that sort of thing. And I've always had the theory that cartoonists shouldn't venture out in public too much, talking. They should stay at home and sit behind the drawing board, drawing. But recently I relented as a special favour to a close friend and found myself in front of a kindergarten class. The teacher asked me to draw a Snoopy on the chalkboard. Now all my life I've always wanted to draw on a big chalkboard. When I was a little kid in school you never got to draw on the chalkboard—you had to stand up there in front of the class and make a fool out of yourself doing geometry on it, but you never got to draw. This was my chance to draw on a beautiful big green chalkboard. So I drew one of my great Snoopys, turned around and said, "Well, what do you think?" One little kid stood up and said, "Can't you draw a better one than that?"

YES, MA'AM, I'M READY...

FOR MY NATURE REPORT TODAY, I AM BRINGING YOU AN EXCLUSIVE!

ROCK SNAKES!!

WHAT, YOU MAY ASK, IS A ROCK SNAKE? THAT IS A GOOD QUESTION! A ROCK SNAKE IS A SNAKE THAT SNEAKS UP BEHIND YOU, AND THROWS A ROCK AT YOU!

NOW, HERE IS MY EXCLUSIVE....IT USED TO BE THOUGHT THAT ROCK SNAKES WERE DANGEROUS, BUT MY AUTHORITY SAYS THIS IS NOT SO...

A ROCK SNAKE CANNOT THROW VERY HIGH, YOU SEE, SO THEREFORE, ALL HE CAN DO IS HIT YOU ON THE BACK OF THE LEG...SO SAYS MY AUTHORITY!

MA'AM?

LINUS VAN PELT.... YES, MA'AM..

SHE SAID SHE REMEMBERS YOU FROM WHEN YOU WERE IN HER CLASS!

ECCLESIASTES.. THIRD CHAPTER..

AH! JUST THE PERSON I WANTED TO SEE...

"TO EVERY THING THERE IS A SEASON," CHARLIE BROWN...

"A TIME TO BE BORN, AND A TIME TO DIE"

"A TIME TO PLANT, AND A TIME TO PLUCK UP THAT WHICH IS PLANTED"

"A TIME TO WEEP, AND A TIME TO LAUGH..A TIME TO MOURN, AND A TIME TO DANCE.."

"A TIME TO LOVE, AND A TIME TO HATE.. A TIME OF WAR, AND A TIME OF PEACE"

AAUGH!

WHAM!

AND A TIME TO PULL AWAY THE FOOTBALL

SCHULZ

I have been able to do things with Snoopy that others hadn't been able to do. It really grew out of the business of people actually talking to their dogs — even answering for them in a form of baby talk. I put in Snoopy's mind the thoughts we sometimes think the dog might be thinking.

I had observed that there were many neighbourhood dogs that seemed almost smarter than the children who were their masters. The dogs seemed to tolerate the silly things the kids did; they seemed to be very wise. This was one of the initial themes of Snoopy which I have built upon in many ways.

Snoopy refuses to be caught in the trap of doing ordinary things like chasing and retrieving sticks and he refuses to take seriously his role as the devoted dog who greets his master when he returns home from school.

I like Snoopy and probably wouldn't mind having him for my own dog, although I sometimes feel as Charlie Brown does when he says, "Why can't I have a normal dog like everyone else?"

It was a dark and stormy night.

Suddenly, out of the mist a spooky figure appeared.

How spooky was he?

Spooooooooky!

I HATE TO TELL YOU THIS, BUT YOUR DINNER IS GOING TO BE ABOUT FOUR MINUTES LATE..

Like all great writers, I have known suffering.

DON'T YOU THINK IT WOULD BE GREAT IF ANIMALS COULD TALK?

HARDLY! I HAVE NO DESIRE TO LISTEN TO SOME BORING TALK FROM THAT STUPID DOG OF YOURS!

WHAT IF I JUST SAID "HAVE A NICE DAY"?

SNOOPY, THE TEACHER SAYS IF YOU'RE GOING TO STAY IN CLASS, YOU'LL HAVE TO SIT WAY IN THE BACK BY YOURSELF...

IF SHE ASKS ME TO SPELL "MISSISSIPPI," I'M IN TROUBLE..

SORRY, THE PUNCH LINE WENT RIGHT OVER MY HEAD!

I COULD HAVE BEEN A SLED DOG, OR MAYBE A PAMPERED PET OF SOME RICH LADY LIVING IN A TOWN HOUSE, OR MAYBE A SHEEP DOG IN AUSTRALIA..

TRUE..FALSE..
TRUE..FALSE..

TRUE..TRUE..
FALSE..TRUE..

HOW ARE YOU DOING?

NO PEEKING!

HE DID **WHAT**?

SHE SAYS YOU GOT THE ONLY PERFECT SCORE ON THE "TRUE OR FALSE" TEST!

NO, MA'AM, I DON'T KNOW HOW HE DID IT..

WHAT'S TRUE IS TRUE, AND WHAT'S FALSE IS FALSE..

Snoopy's appearance and personality have changed probably more than those of any of the other characters. As my drawing style loosened, Snoopy was able to do more things and when I finally developed the formula of using his imagination to dream of being many heroic figures, the strip took on a completely new dimension.

IF YOU GET LOST IN THE WOODS, ONE THING YOU CAN DO IS CLIMB TO THE TOP OF A TREE TO SEE WHERE YOU ARE..

CONRAD WILL NOW DEMONSTRATE FOR US HOW THIS IS DONE...

EXCUSE ME..

I HAVE A QUESTION FOR YOU

IF THERE ARE ALREADY 700,000 ATTORNEYS IN THIS COUNTRY, WHY DO WE NEED YOU?

ATTORNEYS HATE QUESTIONS LIKE THAT!

I IMAGINE THE LIFE OF A SURGEON CAN BE VERY REWARDING..

OBVIOUSLY, YOU HAVE SAVED THE LIVES OF MANY PEOPLE...

IS THAT WHAT LED YOU TO BECOME A SURGEON?

NO, I JUST LIKED THE LITTLE GREEN BOOTIES!

ALL RIGHT, MEN, THIS IS GOING TO BE A LONG HARD MARCH..

FORT ZINDERNEUF IS AT LEAST A HUNDRED MILES AWAY..ARE THERE ANY QUESTIONS?

WHY DON'T WE TAKE A 747?

SERGEANTS IN THE FOREIGN LEGION DON'T ANSWER QUESTIONS LIKE THAT!

When characters work in a comic strip, it is because one thing leads to another and the very personality that you have given him or her starts to provide you with more ideas.

The fussier Lucy became, the more ideas she gave me. Her persecution of poor Linus after he came along, accounted for years and years of ideas. Then came their little brother, Rerun. At first I was sorry I had brought him in. All I could think of doing with him was placing him on the back of his mother's bicycle. Lately, however, I have put him in kindergarten, which was probably inspired by our own grandchildren.

Suddenly, Lucy's personality has mellowed and she has become the only Peanuts character to pay much attention to him. We have seen her playing games with Rerun and actually trying to teach him a few things, but directly opposite of the outrageous teachings she used to push upon Linus.

Rerun Van Pelt is often mistaken for Linus, even though he's his little brother. He can always be recognised in his trademark overalls.

Rerun is more sceptical than his brother, much harder to convince and always gets around Lucy where Linus gives in.

Rerun also longs for a dog of his own, but since his parents won't let him have one, he tries to "borrow" Snoopy from Charlie Brown. Snoopy won't have any part of it unless Rerun brings cookies.

**WHAT ARE YOU DOING OUT HERE?**

**WAITING FOR MY NEW DOG..**

**HOW DO YOU THINK HE'S EVER GOING TO FIND YOU?**

**DOGS ARE SMART.. THEY CAN FIND THEIR WAY ANYPLACE..THEY ALWAYS KNOW WHERE THEY ARE..**

**I THINK I LIVE AROUND HERE SOMEPLACE..**

**RERUN, IT'S TIME FOR SCHOOL! WHERE ARE YOU?**

**I'M NOT GOING! I'M HIDING UNDER MY BED..**

**YOU'D BETTER COME OUT..WHAT'S DAD GONNA SAY?**

**HE UNDERSTANDS.. HE SAID WHEN HE WAS LITTLE, HE HID UNDER THE BED FOR THREE DAYS..**

**ALL RIGHT, STAY THERE! WHAT DO I CARE?**

**NO, MA'AM, MY LITTLEST BROTHER ISN'T STARTING SCHOOL TODAY..HE'S HIDING UNDER HIS BED..**

**I'VE KNOWN TOO MANY PEOPLE WHO WENT TO KINDERGARTEN, AND NEVER AMOUNTED TO ANYTHING..**

Strip 1:
- I HEARD RERUN DIDN'T START KINDERGARTEN LAST WEEK..
- NO, HE HID UNDER THE BED..
- I WONDER IF HE'LL TRY IT AGAIN..
- MAYBE HE'LL FIND SOMEPLACE ELSE TO HIDE..

Strip 2:
- YES, MA'AM .. MY NAME IS "RERUN"... I DON'T KNOW .. THAT'S WHAT THEY ALL CALL ME..
- YES, I KNOW I SHOULD HAVE BEEN HERE LAST WEEK.. WELL, I'M HERE NOW..
- I HOPE WE DON'T HAVE TO READ "WAR AND PEACE" THE FIRST DAY..

Strip 3:
- GUESS WHAT I LEARNED IN SCHOOL TODAY..
- I LEARNED HOW TO WRITE MY NAME..
- NOW I CAN SIGN CHECKS!

Strip 4:
- THIS LITTLE GIRL IN MY CLASS WAS SORT OF DEPRESSED, SEE, SO I SAID, "WHY DON'T WE RUN AWAY TO PARIS?" IT WAS A JOKE
- SHE THOUGHT IT WAS FUNNY SO SHE TOLD HER MOTHER, WHO TOLD OUR TEACHER, WHO TOLD THE PRINCIPAL, AND I GOT FIRED!
- SUSPENDED
- I GUESS SO..
- HARASSMENT?
- STUPIDITY!

Why does Lucy pull away the football every time Charlie Brown comes running up to kick it, and why does he let himself be fooled so often? Obviously, she has a mean streak in her and he has a trusting personality, but readers can certainly see other bits of symbolism there if they wish.

Of course, it all started with memories of our own games, when we were about that age. It was absolutely impossible for anyone to hold the ball on the kickoff. The urge to pull it away was irresistible. Maybe this is what drives Lucy. She really can't help herself. Perhaps she is also annoyed that it is all too easy. Charlie Brown isn't that much of a challenge.

To be consistent, however, we have to let her triumph, for all the loves in the strip are unrequited; all the baseball games are lost; all the test grades are D-minuses; the Great Pumpkin never comes and the football is always pulled away.

In 1965, the class I graduated with was planning its twenty-fifth reunion. I was on the list of people they didn't know what had happened to.

# A *Peanuts* Chronology

## 1950

*Peanuts* daily strip debuts with Charlie Brown, Snoopy, Shermy, and Patty in seven newspapers on October 2.

## 1951

Schroeder is introduced.

## 1952

*Peanuts* Sunday page debuts on January 6.
Lucy and Linus make their first appearances.
First book collection, *Peanuts*, published by Rinehart.

## 1955

Charles M. Schulz receives National Cartoonists Society Reuben Award.

## 1958

Yale University names Schulz Cartoonist of the Year.

## 1959

Sally enters strip.

## 1960

School Bell Award from National Education Society.
Hallmark introduces series of *Peanuts* greeting cards.

## 1961

Frieda introduced into strip.

## 1962

*Happiness Is a Warm Puppy* published by Determined Publications.
Best Humour Strip of the Year Award from National Cartoonists Society.

## 1963

Honorary degree from Anderson College, Anderson, Indiana.

## 1964

*The Gospel According to Peanuts*, by Robert Short, published by John Knox Press.
Second Reuben awarded Charles Schulz by National Cartoonists Society.

# A *Peanuts* Chronology

## 1965

*Peanuts* featured on cover of *Time* magazine (April 9).
Television Special *A Charlie Brown Christmas* wins Emmy and Peabody Awards.
Snoopy appears in first Red Baron sequence (October 10).

## 1966

Snoopy's doghouse burns – he receives many letters of condolence.
Peppermint Patty enters strip.
Schulz receives Honorary Doctor of Humane Letters from St. Mary's College, California.
Television Special *It's the Great Pumpkin, Charlie Brown*.

## 1967

Certificate of Merit awarded by Art Director's Club of New York.
Snoopy and Charlie Brown featured on the cover of *Life* magazine (March 17).
*You're a Good Man, Charlie Brown* opened off Broadway on March 7, and ran for four years.

## 1968

Snoopy joins Manned Flight Awareness Program.
Franklin enters strip.

## 1969

Snoopy and Charlie Brown accompany astronauts into space aboard Apollo X.
Lucy and Snoopy featured on the cover of *Saturday Review* (April 12).
The Redwood Empire Ice Arena in Santa Rosa is opened.

## 1970

Woodstock introduced into strip.
Snoopy joins the Ice Follies.

## 1971

June 17: *Peanuts* Day in San Diego – Charles M. Schulz given key to the city.
Snoopy publishes *It Was a Dark and Stormy Night* (Holt, Rinehart and Winston).
Marcie enters strip.
Snoopy, Charlie Brown, Linus, Lucy and Woodstock on cover of *Newsweek*.
Snoopy joins *Holiday on Ice*.

## 1972

Rerun introduced into strip.
Ice Follies television show – *Snoopy's International Ice Follies*.

# A *Peanuts* Chronology

## 1973

Charles Schulz given Big Brother of the Year Award in San Francisco.
U.S. government uses Snoopy as Energy Conservation Symbol.
Television special *A Charlie Brown Thanksgiving* earns an Emmy Award for
Charles M. Schulz as writer of the show.

## 1974

Schulz is Grand Marshal of the Tournament of Roses Parade, Pasadena.

## 1975

Spike introduced into strip.
Television Special *You're a Good Sport, Charlie Brown* wins Emmy Award.

## 1976

Television Special *Happy Anniversary, Charlie Brown* wins Emmy Award.

## 1978

International Pavilion of Humour, Montreal, names Schulz Cartoonist of the Year.

## 1980

Television Special *Life Is a Circus, Charlie Brown* wins Emmy Award.

## 1983

Television Special *What Have We Learned, Charlie Brown?* wins a Peabody Award for
"distinguished and meritorious public service in broadcasting."
Camp Snoopy opens at Knott's Berry Farm, Buena Park, California.

## 1984

*Peanuts* strip sold to 2,000th newspaper and recorded by Guinness Book of World Records.

## 1985

Oakland Museum opens *Peanuts* exhibit, *The Graphic Art of Charles Schulz.*

## 1986

Lydia enters strip.

## 1989

Publication of Charles M. Schulz's authorized biography, *Good Grief*, by Rheta Grimsley
Johnson.

# A *Peanuts* Chronology

## 1990

Charles M. Schulz receives *Ordre des Arts et des Lettres* from the French Ministry of Culture.
In Paris, the Louvre presents the *Snoopy in Fashion*: exhibit.
The National Museum of History in Washington, D.C. opens.
*This is Your Childhood, Charlie Brown – Children in America Culture. 1945-1970*

## 1992

The Montreal Museum of Fine Art exhibits *Snoopy, the Masterpiece*.
The Italian Minister of Culture awards the Order of Merit to Charles M. Schulz.

## 1995

*Around the Moon and Home Again: A Tribute to the Art of Charles M. Schulz* at the Space Centre in Houston celebrates the strip's 45th anniversary.
A&E Biography features *Charles Schulz – A Charlie Brown Life*.

## 1996

Star is placed on Hollywood's Walk of Fame in honour of Charles M. Schulz.

## 1997

World premiere at Carnegie Hall of *Peanuts Gallery*, by composer Ellen Taaffe Zwilich.

## 1998

The Little Red-Haired Girl finally appears, but just as a silhouette, dancing with Snoopy.

## 1999

*You're a Good Man, Charlie Brown* opens new production on Broadway.

## 2000

February 12: Charles M. Schulz, aged 77, who had been suffering from colon cancer, died in his sleep.
October 2: *Peanuts* 50th Anniversary.